Renew Your Wows:

Seven Powerful Tools to Ignite the Spark and Transform Your Relationship

Jeffrey H. Sumber

RAINDROPS PRESS

CHICAGO

All the business names, product names, and brand names used within this book are trademarks, trade names, or registered trademarks of their respective owners. The author is not associated with any product, business entity, or company. The views, opinions, and strategies in this book are purely those of the author.

Limit of Liability/ Disclaimer of Warranty: While the publisher and author have used their best efforts in preparing this book, they make no representations or warranties with respect to the accuracy or completeness of the contents of this book and specifically disclaim any implied warranties of merchantability or fitness for a particular purpose. No warranty may be created or extended by sales representatives or written sales materials. The advice and strategies contained herein may not be suitable to your situation, particular state of mental health, or treatment with a licensed professional. Consult with a professional mental health clinician where appropriate. Neither the publisher nor the author shall be liable for any loss of profit or any commercial, professional or clinical damages, including but not limited to special, incidental, consequential, or other damages.

Although the author and publisher have made every effort to ensure that the information contained herein is correct at press time, the author and publisher do not assume and hereby disclaim any liability to any party for any loss, damage, or disruption caused by errors or omissions, whether such errors or omissions result from negligence, accident, or any other cause. While every effort is made to ensure that all the information in this book is accurate and up to date, we accept no responsibility for keeping the information up to date or any liability for any failure to do so.

"There are so many books about doing relationships 'right' yet so few of them focus on doing "you" right first. Jeffrey Sumber understands that the foundation of any healthy couple rests in healthy individuals. *Renew Your Wows* takes us on a journey of self-discovery that is both powerful and hopeful. This is the best 'self-recovery' book I've read in a long time."

—Michelle Phillips, Author of
The Beauty Blueprint, TV personality,
and radio host

"*Renew Your Wows* is one of those books that forces us to look deep within and ponder the places we lost sight of Love's passionate embrace. The difference here is that Jeffrey Sumber shows us the way back to that alchemy. It is a beautiful, awakening journey."

—Arjuna Ardagh, Author of *Better Than Sex*
and founder of Awakening Coaching

"The first time I met Jeffrey Sumber I had the great pleasure of witnessing he and his beautiful wife mindfully meander and intermittently giggle through the labyrinth here at the Sacred Garden on Maui. When I read his book, it all clicked. Here is a man who is playful and wise, open and conscious, and that is how *Renew Your Wows* comes across to the reader. The process of renewal that Sumber maps out for us is profoundly beautiful because it is an authentic reflection of life and the winding path it sometimes leads us through deep into our relationships."

—Eve Eschner Hogan, Author of *The EROS Equation: A Soul-ution for Relationships* and owner of *Heart Path Journeys* Retreats on Maui

"Jeffrey Sumber has captured the essence and potential simplicity of being in relationship with others, transcending our learned habits of blame, judgment, and 'make-wrong' of others close to us. In a real way, Jeffrey lives from his heart. An 18-year old Native American woman once told me, 'Everything in life is about relationship.' Jeffrey and his writings affirm this."

— *Dr. Bruce Scott,* Psychologist and acclaimed author of *Being Real* and *Free the Children*

"Jeffrey Sumber brings clarity to the morass of modern coupledom. His solutions are compassionate and wise."

— Pamela Druckerman, Author of *Bringing Up Bébé*

"I have had the pleasure of learning about relationships and intimacy from Jeffrey for several years now and what inspires me most about him, his work, and this book, is that it is authentic. HE is authentic. He doesn't pretend to know it all or have it all figured out, because the truth is, we all need to find our own paths. I found mine, partly in and through conversations with him — and made the decision to leave a 12-year relationship. Now I am in the process of exploring and re-defining what I want and need from a partnership and these tools no doubt form part of my learning and journey to being a more authentic lover and partner, getting ready to fall in love head-over-heels once more."

— Jana Schuberth, Founder and Director of *Alive in Berlin,* international coach, teacher, and digital nomad

"I highly recommend this book to my clients, friends, and people I mentor because it facilitates an even more amazing life! If you need a little help with your relationship, this is your first stop. The companion workbook is worth its weight in gold and makes the ideas and exercises come to life in such a way that you really can't resist introducing some shifts into your life."

—Scott Armstrong, Best-selling author of
Boston Marathon or Bust and Founder of
Boulder Coaching Academy

"*Renew Your Wows* will wow you into a greater understanding of yourself and your relationship, while also giving you the tools and techniques you need to bring back the passion, playfulness, and excitement you're missing together. I warmly recommend it to all my clients, mentees, and friends who are longing for deeper and more rewarding connections. The seven tools in this book will lead you through great transformation, not only in your close relationships, but in the rest of your life as well!"

—Marthe Hagen, Author of
Feeling Good When Life is Hard,
international coach, and blogger

"*Renew Your Wows* offers potent practices that help couples shift the conflicts of relationship past cycles of blame and resentment into mutual insight and shared empowerment. In this focused, no-nonsense guide, Sumber manages to help couples rekindle the depths of their love of self and of each other."

—Galen Fous MTP, Renowned sex
researcher and author of *Adult Sex Ed for 21st
Century Sexuality* (Fall 2015)

"Jeffrey Sumber has created a practical, heartfelt book that gives shape and guidance to that which so many of us seek: Manifesting and keeping a healthy, loving relationship with ourselves and someone else. Drawing upon his own and others' personal experiences, Sumber has created an excellent guidebook that uses real life situations and examples that you can relate to while providing enough space and creativity for you to make it work in your own life. Keep this on a low bookshelf because you'll be reaching for it often!"

— Dr. Frankie Bashan, Lesbian matchmaker, psychotherapist and relationship coach

Why This Book?

You and I have floated here on the stream
that brings from the fount.
At the heart of time, love of one for another.
We have played alongside millions of lovers, shared in the same
Shy sweetness of meeting, the same distressful tears of farewell-
Old love but in shapes that renew and renew forever.

Today it is heaped at your feet, it has found its end in you
The love of all... days both past and forever:
Universal joy, universal sorrow, universal life.
The memories of all loves merging with this one love of ours –
And the songs of every poet past and forever.

— R. Tagore

Your life is meant to be poetry. The way you feel when you just fall in love with someone is the way you're meant to feel about yourself when you wake up each day.

Renew Your Vows: Seven Powerful Tools to Ignite the Spark and Transform Your Relationship is written for individuals, yet is geared to help relationships sing again. With a significant focus on your personal journey to understand life and love, this is less a relationship "diet" book of "do this" and "don't do that" and more about a creative lifestyle change.

Renew Your Vows is a book for the Selves in every Couple. It's written with simple tools to plug right into your daily life. Whether you're singing in the rain together or gritting your teeth and rolling your eyes, this book provides you with a roadmap to reframe your relationship experience and grow deeper as individuals so you can wake up smiling again.

A great deal of love went into the writing of this book. I have a deep appreciation for relationships and a significant personal investment in the subject. The content that follows is my own integration of some of the most cutting edge theories and research in my field blended with my own experiences and observations.

Are you ready to change the game and *Renew your Wows?*

Dedication

This book is dedicated to everyone I have ever offered love to and from whom I have had the gift of receiving love.

Still, there is no one I can acknowledge more meaningfully as a researcher than my Self.

I am constantly challenged by old patterns, old thoughts, and behaviors that tempt me to curse it all and abandon my deepest Self. Still, I rise each day and challenge the Siren's call to crash against the rocks.

Love is at once profoundly seductive and grotesquely repelling. It does not offer its gift without the residue of shadow and so we dance until the morning light when the shadow and the light become one.

I wake each day and choose relationship.

Contents

Introduction

I feel like I hate relationships almost as much as I sit in awe of them. Not only do my own relationships occasionally kick my ass, but I also work as a relationship consultant with many brave couples each month which provides its own challenges. The thousands of people I've worked with over the past two decades have taught me that so many of us often find ourselves in "the Soup," that steaming pot of hot liquid relationship mess. In the Soup, instead of moving *closer* to our partners because we desperately want the connection reestablished, we often go the wrong way! It's almost like we can't stop ourselves. We humans have an uncanny tendency to start adding ingredients to our simple broth until we have a hearty pot of relationship stew. This is hard to digest.

Most of the time, life inside the world of a couple is wonderful. There are beautiful memories full of giggles and winks, passion, and winter binge-watching afternoons. And still, there are few experiences in life that can leave us feeling as powerless, and as stuck, as our relationships. Whether it's the silent treatment, the bickering, the months of trekking through the sexual tundra, or, my personal favorite, the "Fuck It!" button where we simply say, "what's the point, let's just end this here and now," relationships are not easy work. Even as an expert in my field, I *still* have moments of extreme difficulty finding the "That Was Easy" button.

Regardless of whether you've been together a month or an eternity, we all need a sense of renewal in our meaningful partnerships. But here's the good news- you don't have to suffer in the Soup any longer than it takes to read this book.

There's a story I like to tell of a monk who leaves his monastery to live alone in a cave, believing it will lead to enlightenment. The other monks from the monastery deliver a wooden bowl of simple food for him at the mouth of the cave each morning so he doesn't have to worry about anything except meditating (and becoming really skinny). After 20 years, the monk decides that he has, indeed, attained nirvana, the state of profound bliss and non-attachment. He emerges from his self-imposed exile, going forth into the world of bumbling idiots to teach the way of transcendence in hopes that the rest of us can stop bickering and sabotaging our lives.

In town, a rickshaw driver runs over his toe with a shoddy wooden wheel. The monk, losing his cool, begins swearing at him. (Imagine if they had cell phone cameras back then- he'd be trending on all the lists.) In that moment, he realizes he won't ever attain enlightenment unless he creates it in the space of relationship with others.

In other words, nothing matters in a cave and everything matters in the context of our relationships. Perhaps this is why so many men like to hide in their man caves. Sure, it's a relaxing retreat, and we all need to recharge. However, who among us has never used it, or something like it, as a way to hide from the work of intimacy, attachment, and relationship?

As a seasoned therapist, there are moments I feel as naïve and humbled as the monk who just wants to return to his safe bubble of omniscience and not be discouraged by the messy nature of coupling, yours or mine. So why would you buy a book from a guy who admits that his relationship sometimes feels like a quagmire, just like yours? That's a great question.

The answer is that my relationships, and my clients' relationships, have improved significantly over the years as a result of the processes and ideas revealed in this book. My ability to manage the ups and downs of coupling has changed with the tools I've adopted and I find myself longing for my cave less and less. While it's true I still occasionally find myself in the Soup, I can see myself in my own dance- I can see the spots more easily where I can, and do, jump off the wild ride.

Now, any expert who suggests they can "fix" your relationship is, quite frankly, off their rocker. On the other hand, we can certainly help get you and your partner in much better shape. That's the promise of this book. To do this, all you need is to be fed up and ready to change the situation in which you find yourself.

One of the secrets of having a relationship that works is to learn how to focus your negative attention on the things that keep you from living happily with your partner– *not on your partner*. The path of self-realization and personal growth is really about this question:

> *Who do I want to be and am I able to live from that intention in relationship with others?*

Every relationship you have – business, friendship, family, or romantic love – can help you find the answers to that question, but only one, by its very nature, offers us the most potential on the path to being our best selves. No matter how many books on self-growth, mating, reproducing, conscious coupling, or Tantra and the endless orgasm, you may have read, there is still one path in life that offers you the best shot at true self-awareness, compassion, and deep contentedness.

You know the one.

It's the one you go to bed with at night and wake up to in the morning. Maybe you've married them, maybe you haven't. Maybe you're on the fence. Heck, maybe you're even considering ending it right now. Regardless, when the truth is told, existing in the tension of a committed relationship is one of the greatest teachers you will ever know. Your partner can be the one who hangs the stars for you and, just as easily, be the source of your disgust and misery when you don't get what you want.

Who better to push your buttons and challenge you than a long-term partner?

No, it's not always fun — especially when you consider we tend to choose people who make us deeply happy *and* piss us off more than others. But there's a divine wisdom to that, an intuitive "method to the madness," you might say.

So, how do you take the good with the bad and make sense of it all? How do you make sense of your own ability to be the cheesiest, nerdiest, goofiest ball of seventh heaven *and* the meanest, coldest, detached sociopath one can imagine-oftentimes in the same day?

Falling in love is a magical, spiritual, physically altering event. Staying in love is work. Staying in love is not about *hoping* your love will renew itself, it's about taking the deep journey inside yourself and identifying who you are, what you truly want, and what practical steps will get you there. Relationships are not "separate" entities like so many of us like to claim. Your relationship is about you and it's about him or her. It's about how you're feeling about yourself, what degree of projection you're living in, and the degree to which you're taking true ownership of getting your needs met. It's about personal responsibility. The solution to relationship success is focusing inward not outward. It's not about them — it's about you.

The process described in this book arose from my own desire to make the relationships in my life work. It didn't matter that I'd studied at some of the best schools in the world and received mentoring from some of the world's most acclaimed psychologists, coaches, and master relationship teachers, I still faced my own challenges at home.

After too many discussions arguing over what percentage of my relationship was amazing and how much was utter trash, I decided I had to do something different. It was that or the fear that "I'd be better off alone" would take over for good. If you're anything like me, or the hundreds of couples I work with each year who sit on my couch and say, "when we're good, we're really good, but 10-15% of the time it's pretty much the worst relationship I've ever experienced. I mean, it's *terrible!*"

It took me a long time and lots of practice to understand what this percentage thing is really about for many people. Somewhere, somehow, we've come to believe that if a relationship is "right" it must be smooth sailing, easy, loving, and passionate 99% of the time. Surely anything less must be an indication of faulty coupling, right? Typically, it's when you're in one of those moments of 15-20% misery that you look across to your partner and decide, *"you are the reason I'm not happy."* I get it — it's hard not to go there. And yet, we couldn't be further from the truth.

I've received degrees from great institutions, including Harvard, and found there is no effective scholarship out there that actually changes everything when you and your partner are in the Soup. The reality is that nothing fixes everything. That being said, this book *will* make a profound difference in the quality of your relationship if you work with the ideas and tools I suggest.

There are seven tools I use, and teach my clients to use, on a regular basis that will help you renew your wows:

The Seven Tools to Renew Your Wows
1. Uncovering the Self
2. Where Do I Live? Paradigm GPS
3. Respond Instead of React
4. Reject Projection and Assert Responsibility
5. The Check-In Dialogue
6. Processing the Rules of Engagement
7. Separate Facts from Feelings

Each of these tools is described fully in the following chapters. What I've found while working with couples and individuals throughout my career is that the vast majority of us simply want to be happy, yet part of why we get so insanely frustrated in relationships is because we see ourselves making the very decisions that keep us stuck. We all know that saying something critical or mean to our partner in the heat of an argument will likely cause damage and keep us in a negative cycle even longer. We understand that the words we use matter; however we continue to make poor choices. We *know* with every fiber of our beings that we should be leaps and bounds better at this silly relationship thing and still, we struggle.

So, what's the secret? Why do so many of the couples I work with tend to find their way out of the dark? What has twenty years of working with wondrous relationships taught me? It isn't so much about a secret as it is about the execution of the tools. You can have a really good sense as to what "types" you both might be and how that plays into giving or receiving love, yet unless there's a safe, practical process that serves as the shock absorber whenever it all hits the fan, all the self-help books in the world won't save the day. All of the great relationship books throughout time and space won't do you any good unless you and your partner can put a handful of proven strategies and solutions into play when you are actively hating, feeling disgusted, feeling repulsed, feeling numb or are completely stuck in "fight or flight" mode. So, how is this even possible?

These seven tools are simple strategies, hacks even, to convince the system of your relationship that it can accept common sense in the middle of a dramatic battle sequence. Think of a romantic comedy set in a war zone. The bullets and bombs are flying left and right, yet suddenly our beautiful couple pauses to acknowledge the agreed upon relational rules of engagement. These tools help to shift the landscape of your emotional exchanges by anticipating the reality that you will not only find yourself in the Soup, undoubtedly before you know it, but that the Soup is just soup. The power of your need for each other and the intensity of your desire to love and receive love can help to place the fight or flight defense mechanism on the shelf and get back to the business of enjoying life.

These seven simple tools allow you to re-contextualize the drama of the negative exchange with your partner into a basic equation that exists in an alternate reality from the one you are so accustomed to being kicked around by; a relational dimension where feelings replace more transactional, cognitive ones and zeroes. Couples who want to feel good about their inherent relationship skills and utilize this framework for diffusing the bombs threatening their daily sense of happiness experience more moments of happiness than they imagined possible before adopting this process. While the tools are rooted in some old and new theory, they're discussed here in very basic terms. To help solidify the concepts, you'll also find *Inspired Actions* at the end of certain chapters to help you further integrate the material.

Like many of my clients, I spent much of my life projecting onto others to get my needs met and to explain why I wasn't happy, which, of course, was because others were not meeting and fulfilling my needs. At least that's what I told myself. In one case it was a spiritual teacher who was supposed to enlighten me but wouldn't. Another time, it was a financial planner who was supposed to make me more money- he blamed the markets. In my romantic relationship, my girlfriend was supposed to fulfill me sexually and emotionally, but didn't (or worse, wouldn't). It's these kinds of expectations that occur all too often in relationships and, for the most part, are the basis of unhappiness.

As we move forward, it's important to remember that a relationship does not *fail*, it either supports you and your growth or it creates pain and disappointment leading to a state of sadness and frustration. Failure would suggest that you did not learn or grow at all, and that's highly unlikely. The funny thing is that both states of being can be consciously true in the same day. *This is one of the most important points of this book.* When you operate from a premise of good or bad, pass or fail, then you'll inevitably start keeping score, comparing what's happening to past and projected statistics.

Sometimes in an effort to escape the negative feelings, people create self-defeating strategies. For example, during the first ten years of my adult life, I had this great idea of transcending my body and becoming enlightened, like the monk in the story. My goal was to become so spiritual that I wouldn't need to be in my body anymore. This made perfect sense to me. My partner at the time had a strong desire to have sex with people other than myself and while it made my stomach turn, I tried to convince myself that if I was spiritual enough, it would no longer bother me! Great strategy- except it didn't work. You can't escape negative feelings by overlooking deeper issues or by overwhelming them with pure, unadulterated bliss, hoping it will wash away your pain and sadness and replace it with oneness.

In the end, I realized this was a self-defeating approach to my situation and that almost an entire decade of my life had been devoted to something I now warmly refer to as a "spiritual bypass." Psychologist John Welwood coined the term back in the 1980's to explain how some people use the spiritual path as a way to ignore unresolved emotional, relational and/or psychological issues. Unfortunately I didn't get the memo until after I had taken a few detours. You don't have to take that long. One of my goals in writing this book is to give you a shortcut that can strip years away from the learning curve. In fact, I have created a companion Action Guide that will accompany you on this journey through renewing your wows. Download the action guide (you will find the link to your free copy in the Appendix) and after each tool is discussed in the book, you will find a corresponding set of exercises in the workbook that makes the process easier to integrate and probably more fun.

Maybe you thought she would be like a porn star in bed with you, but would never think of cheating on you when she left the house in the morning. Perhaps you believed he would be the "good guy" who would never leave you home alone on a weekend night to be with the guys and would know how to masterfully fix every moving part in your house. They were supposed to fulfill all of your unmet and unspoken needs and match a good number of your fantasies to boot. But they fell short. She doesn't even like oral sex and he eventually called a plumber to fix the sink (that he "repaired" three times) on his way to poker night.

If you're reading this book, you probably feel like most of the couples I work with- stuck. A sense of hopelessness has come to fill the holes that have started to puncture the euphoria you used to enjoy, especially in the beginning of your relationship. Here are some of the complaints I hear:

> *"We used to love each other, and now I just don't feel like we're there, and we don't even know how to get there anymore."*

> *"I'm not even sure anymore if this was ever good. Was I delusional?"*

> *"She used to love sex and now it's like she could go on forever without it and never bring it up."*

> *"I feel like I was sold a bill of goods here. This is not the person I fell in love with. This is not the person I walked down the aisle with."*

If this sounds familiar, you've come to the right place.

The dance of negative cycles can spin a relationship into such chaos that the damage seems irrevocable. Yet, what we are desperately shouting for is to love and be loved, to feel safe within the context of the relationship, and to feel that the majority of our core needs are being met. It's not about a return to the way things used to be, but rather the creation of a new home where you work together to build a place in which you can both feel safe, connected, and nurtured.

I guarantee that after you have completed this book, your life will look and feel different. You will marvel at the relationship, where previously you referred to it as "fine" or "I don't know anymore." New practices will pepper your old routines with fresh possibilities and establish a new paradigm for your relationship. In picking up this book, it's obvious you already have an investment in living the kind of life that you know is your destiny.

What's that, you say? You would rock that reality if it weren't for the dead weight on the other side of the table? The man or woman who sold you a bill of goods back in the day?

Consider this:

*Why would you want to be with the same person
you knew years ago?*

The thought of existing in the same framework you both created long ago and projecting it into eternity is a ridiculously bad idea. It's not only a blueprint for discontent, stuck-ness, and restlessness; it's likely a path toward resentment. It keeps us tethered to the confines of an old agreement as to how things are *supposed* to be rather than a dynamic, changing, living entity that supports *who we are becoming*. Why? Because it's rooted in a paradigm that suggests that we do not grow, that we shouldn't challenge each other to become bigger beings and better versions of ourselves. It's a prescription for a plastic, cinematic relationship that never ages, never shifts, and never uncovers more of itself. It's like trying to Botox the relationship. Unfortunately, Botox is not the key to longevity- it's a mask that hides real growth and development.

Still, it's no wonder you feel trapped and frustrated sometimes.

That's why, rather than attempting to re-commit to the vows, understandings, and patterns that kicked off the relationship long ago, I recommend a *renewal of wows*.

This process is one in which we find new pathways to create organic closeness, intimacy, and safety without relying on or pining for the way things used to work. It's time to redesign the landscape by first uncovering the growth that has occurred in the time that has elapsed since you first moved into your emotional starter home. Don't focus on finding out where the person you originally partnered with went; instead, uncover who they have become and who they are still becoming.

What will really bake your biscuit, however, is the first step: figuring out what happened to the person *you* used to be.

Now, that's fun. Let's get started, shall we?

Chapter One

Your New Toolkit

Become a possibilitarian. No matter how dark
things seem to be or actually are, raise your sights and
see possibilities -- always see them, for they're
always there.

— Dr. Norman Vincent Peale

Ben Franklin was more than a brilliant statesman and
founding father, he was also a well known scientist and
inventor. In fact, some of his inventions are still widely used
today. One such gift from this brilliant Quaker was the
lightening rod. What a relief it was, and continues to be, that
we don't have to run to the store and buy a new flat screen
every time there's an electrical storm. The reason? A little
gizmo attached to the roof with a huge piece of copper or
aluminum wire running down along the building and into the
ground where it's attached to a conductive grid. The lightning
strikes the rod on the roof and then amazingly seeks the path
of least resistance, which gratefully avoids our expensive stuff
inside. The lightning rod is our best warranty against
electrocution. It also happens to be a great design to help us

not get fried in our relationships! You didn't know Franklin was a relationship guy, too, did you?

Let's consider how the premise of a lightning rod can do a great deal of good in the context of interpersonal connection and interplay. In a relationship, we need a way to ensure that when lightning strikes, and things heat up between us, we will be safe and unharmed. You and I can probably tell plenty of stories about previous relationships where we got burned. Perhaps your partner said something cruel, maybe they cheated or lied and you've become jaded with the idea of trust. Well, Ben Franklin gave us the blueprint so we can save the gems of our personalities and our kind hearts. The relationship lightning rod is the Process. The Process is the dependable, durable, shockproof vessel that keeps the contents of our feelings and experiences intact, safe, and non-toxic. All it takes is one of us to create a safe and consistent process. It definitely works best when both parties utilize the same process, however as long as one of you adheres to the guidelines and structure of the process, you will both benefit.

The process is a collection of ideas and beliefs that lay the foundation for a handful of guidelines and understandings for engagement that the two of you discuss and agree upon when times are simple and sweet. Aside from establishing the basics as to which paradigm the relationship will operate within, for example differentiating between the transactional and process paradigms, there are numerous other components of a healthy relationship that entail a substantial process.

As you'll discover in this book, there is a collection of basic ideas and premises that you'll want to discuss with your partner to set up parameters for healthy interaction. Some of them include:

Projections

Reactions vs. Responses

Appreciations

Needs vs. Expectations

Gifts vs. Presents

For the majority of couples I see, they "get it" in a way that sticks within six to eight weeks of practice. It takes that long for certain behaviors to begin to change and generate more healthy responses, solidifying the paradigm shift. That process then becomes more concrete in two or three months and couples tend to feel significantly better. Remember, metacognition is the way we dig deeper into a particular concept and help make it practice. Process, then, is our practice of thinking about the functioning of our relationship. It's incredibly helpful to understand how your partner thinks and how they generate understanding when it comes to simple and complex thoughts and practices in life.

Don't think for a moment that pondering the nature of relationship is not as vital a function of thought as spatial relations or conceptualizing matter into electrons and protons. In fact, establishing that a partner may not be a natural at sharing his or her feelings actually allows them to develop strategies to do better. You might consider it unromantic using a hack like a pop-up calendar reminder on their mobile phone, for example, that simply states: "share something personal" or "ask how are you feeling right now?" However, folks who lean toward the left side of their brain still have a very healthy right pocket up there, they just need a little encouragement. They need to know that if they take a risk, they'll be safe. While the methodology may not sound romantic and heartfelt, getting your needs met will feel better than questioning the process to get there. Remember, your partner is still meeting your need because they care!

When we understand the areas of the relationship where we need to focus more work, we tend to grow more substantially and meaningfully as a result. While discussing the process in some detail might arguably take some of the magic out of just winging a relationship, the simple fact that the two of you make it a priority and part of your conversation actually raises the bar of your relationship. Most of us desire the prospect of growth in life. We long for a sense of meaning at a very basic level and learning who we are and how we operate in relationships offers us both the opportunity to grow and to feel more solid when it comes to making sense of it all.

A significant component of solidifying your intimate relationship is trusting that your partner is by your side, has your back, and has no desire to hurt you intentionally. You can't really get down to business until you make the time and create the space to build a true, safe bridge between you and your partner. Trust is the precious flour in your favorite, delicious, cake. Yet, you're the one who bakes the cake, not your partner. Their verbalization that they trust you or general reassurance that all will work out is just the icing on the cake. True, cake is always better with icing, but damned if I won't eat a plain cake anyway.

We all have a primal need to feel safe and secure. We also have a deep need to love and feel loved. We want to feel cared about and we want to feel secure enough to take risks in exploring our feelings and expressing our creativity within the context of coupling. Have you and your partner developed the safety and trust that you need to express yourself in an authentic and fulfilling manner? Have you and your partner agreed upon ways to ensure that feelings of intimacy, trust, and security are protected and cherished? Oftentimes, this isn't even possible until the discussion about process has been conducted.

The Process is durable and dependable and like Franklin's Rod (I am officially naming this as Ben Franklin's greatest relationship invention) will keep you safe from great emotional harm if utilized correctly. Without it, you just might get fried. Or worse, you might find yourself lost or stuck or totally numbed out to your own life. David Byrne sang about potentially finding ourselves at the wheel of a large automobile- feeling like, whose life is this, anyway? There's something about that song that reminds me we're at the wheel of our story, the music of our life, and that we can also put it at a distance if not totally disengage from it. We each have our own monologue that we love to share. I'm in a beautiful house, with a beautiful wife (or partner), and all is good until... then we ask ourselves, how did we get here? We have a tendency to perceive our life's circumstances, and even it's totality, from the lens of a particular moment.

When it comes to the dance of our relationships, we learn the steps as we move through our lives but the music changes from moment to moment, forcing us to stay tuned in and responsive to the different rhythms, the highs and lows, the words. It's essential that we remain conscious and present for the playlist so we can dance accordingly. This requires a conscious process of attunement- we tune in to the signals we are getting from each other and do our best to move accordingly.

However, when you're knee deep in quicksand it's rather challenging to believe that the whole planet isn't comprised of the stuff. And yet, this patch of goop is probably only 6 feet by 6 feet with a beautiful forest just out of sight. The challenge is trusting that you'll get out of the pit and that you'll have the ability to view the forest as it truly is and not carry the pit with you into the beautiful planet that is our authentic home.

Though frustrating, the problems we face in our relationship have more to do with ourselves than our partners. If we want to exist within a state of attunement where we generally feel like we get each other and exist in a state of connectedness on multiple levels, the finger we like to point toward the Other must first curl back towards the Self. In order to experience a more vibrant, passionate relationship with your significant other, it's essential to start placing the overall focus of your energy and intention on creating the transformation from within.

It's scary how liberating it can feel once we stop blaming our partner for our own sadness and frustration. Once again, I speak as an expert in blaming my partners many times without any significant progress that I can not stress this one enough. Stop focusing on them and bring back the power of your anger and frustration to replenish your own reservoir of strength. You're going to need that energy to overcome the obstacles inside that are preventing you from truly having the kind of love and safety you not only desire, but actually need, in order to feel whole.

Consider what the Sufi poet, Hafiz, wrote about joy hundreds of years ago, "I caught the happy virus last night when I was out singing beneath the stars. It is remarkably contagious."

The message here is that when we begin to think, feel, and act in alignment with our greatest joy, peace, and emotional well being as our core intention, the world begins to seem a bit more hospitable. Think about the power of walking into your bedroom singing a song you love, full of happiness, and giggling at your own off-key tune. Your partner's already there, waiting for you, and can feel the lightness and goodwill that you're emitting from your pores. This typically isn't a precursor for battle, unless perhaps you're truly a horrible singer and inflict pain on their eardrums.

The kicker to remember here is that you aren't just loving yourself by being yourself, you're also offering your authentic and beautiful nature to your partner. It's a blessing and a gift to them. When you are feeling bad about yourself it's likely that you're warping your picture of reality. We tend to seek affirmation of our terrible ugliness in the eyes and actions of the people we love. If my loving partner thinks my voice is horrific, then it just confirms what I already know. Even so, screw them for thinking so. In fact, if I'm so bad then I might as well push them away now so neither of us has to endure the Kryptonite that most assuredly fills my core. If I start an interaction hating myself, it is safe to say that nothing, *nothing...* that I experience will be based on truth.

Take this example one step further and you'll see how everything experienced under these circumstances will serve as a roadblock to prevent the attainment of a desperately needed home base of safety, connectedness, and healthy attachment. Instead of establishing positive, healthy communication in the context of a safe process, we transmute anything potentially healing into distorted shapes and sounds, which become the landscape of our relationship trajectory. While we might be feeling gross about ourselves, instead of taking the risk of sharing this most vulnerable and potentially unattractive feeling with our partner, we project the whole grossness onto them and either blame them for making us feel disgusting, hurt them, abandon them, or otherwise malign them in some forceful way that establishes even more distance from our desired safe haven. We typically go to war in these moments instead of being creative about getting our needs met. A little diplomacy often saves lives and the life we save may just be our own! Self-loathing makes us doubt everything and oftentimes distorts the real intentions of our partners to the point at which we turn joy, kindness, and pleasure into resentment, expectation, and performance.

> **Conflict is the inflammation that occurs when the virus of emotional disconnection runs rampant in our relationship.**
>
> — Dr. Sue Johnson

So how do we avoid this train-wreck once and for all? We tend to make real movement in our lives when we create (or fall into) new, emotionally-connected behaviors that are well received and warmly returned. This, once again, brings us back to a state of conscious awareness in our agreed upon process and leads us down the road of authentic enjoyment, pleasure, and an appreciation for giving and receiving love. Your partner is with you because they believe you to be better than you think you are. So, when you think you're terrible, you tend to want them to confirm for you what goes against their understanding of the truth. You have a person in your life who wants to express love for you in some way and they should be received as a hero. Gratitude, appreciation and respect are better responses to love than blame and shame. Sometimes trusting that our partner isn't insane is the sanest thing you can do in your relationship. Maybe it's high time you stop trying to get him or her to confirm what a horrible person you are. If you're reading this book, I seriously doubt you are a horrible person.

When faced with perceived danger, humans instinctively go into fight or flight mode. Attachment psychologists of the past century suggest that any loss of safe attachment, closeness, reciprocal intimacy, etc., pose a perceived threat. We are engineered to fight with our neighbors or run from more powerful invaders if we feel the threat is real enough. So it is in our closest relationships. Our instinct is to either attack our partners when they suggest a withdrawal of love or closeness, or to hit the abort button and find someone else who will love us right now. This is biology and not some aberration in *your* unique relationship. As an evolving species, we are invited to assess the danger in the context of what we are truly afraid of. When my partner attacks me for not remembering Valentine's Day or for staring too long at another primate, it's my nature to say "screw you, I'll just go grab my things and leave."

Yet, if I'm being honest, there are many reasons why I feel scared in that moment. I feel bad, for one thing, and perhaps I'm afraid that I really am a jerk. Or even deeper, I really want my partner to love me and help me feel safe and aligned in my life, so that a threat to this security challenges the world I have made peace with in recent days, months, and years. It's perfectly reasonable to panic in these situations. It would be odd if you didn't. Still, some of us have an overall sense of connectedness, but we get stuck in feeling disconnected from a *particular* person and/or a fear of the imminent demise of that particular relationship.

Wait. Hold on a second. Who is this "I" we're talking about, anyway? David Byrne was on to something deep, but he stopped short of spelling it out for his head-bobbing, rock-

and-roll audience. Forget your beautiful wife or your car. Who are *you*? What's *your* story?

A 7-Minute Story

> **Change the way you look at something, and the thing you look at changes.**
> —Wayne Dyer

Try this. Tell the story of your life to someone you know, other than your partner, in seven minutes or less. That's it. Go do it now. Call someone on the phone or grab a stranger walking down the street and share whatever comes out in the allotted time. If you can't find someone, record yourself a voice memo on your smartphone.

There's nothing quite like trying to encapsulate your life in a 7-minute-or-less sound bite in order to get a snapshot of where you're at *now*. Did your story focus on the last 6-months? Did your narrative begin with "I was born on such and such day and in such and such place and had two nannies"? Some people jump straight into emotions like sadness or anger, others stick to facts. Did you stare into your friend's eyes and claim, "I don't know what to say?"

What do we really have to lose in allowing the world to see us as we are? As I see it, nothing. In fact, we have everything to gain, including the most important thing- true connection. Some valuable questions to ask yourself as you consider how you told your story are:

- Am I being a victim?
- What's the story really about today?
- How do I define myself?
- Is my story about suffering?
- Is it about overcoming obstacles?
- Is this an accurate picture of who I am?
- Am I still looking for something that I don't have?
- How did it feel to tell my story?

- Where do relationships factor into my story?
- How does my current relationship situation reflect my past?

Why tell your story just for the sake of repeating it when you can just as easily use it as an opportunity to create new stories and derive more meaning than you have given yourself credit for at times? Instead of using it for feedback, try using it for self-observation.

The stories we tell are important because they relate to our paradigms, our worldviews, and, ultimately, translate into how we see our partners. Is your story that your partner doesn't love you right? Or doesn't have sex enough? Or your partner doesn't help out enough? This is just a tired, old recording of blame which suggests someone is responsible for your happiness. Clearly, this sort of jibber-jabber will never get us what we want, though it does allow us to shirk responsibility for our own joy and place the blame onto someone else.

As we uncover and share our stories of yesterday, we can offer more light, compassion, and understanding to the stories of today.

The power of *witness*, the experience of seeing and/or being seen, cannot be overstated. There is something very significant about being seen and witnessed as yourself, by your partner. Your partner is in a position to see where you're from, what shaped you, and even where you've been hurt.

The deeper you enter the Process Paradigm described throughout these pages with your partner, the easier it becomes for them to separate your past hurts from your current issues with them. This can be very freeing for both partners. It's an invaluable exercise that can reveal the existence of an emotional trigger or "hot spot" that is pre-existing. It doesn't mean these hot spots won't trigger us any longer, however it'll provide more context and understanding while allowing for personal responsibility. The establishment of a healthy, durable process in your relationship requires a process in and of itself! As we journey together in this book, you will learn more and more components that you and your partner can rely upon to keep yourselves out of the Soup. By the time you reach chapter seven and establish a working agreement for the way in which you engage in dialogue, the foundation for process will be obvious and, for many, a relief.

If you, like me, believe that relationships are all about effective, loving, and clear processes, then understanding why and how we get triggered is like seeing the artist's color palette alongside the finished painting. It helps us see where we're from and how we got where we are. This is relationship art.

Renew Your Wows

- The process is a collection of ideas and beliefs that lay the foundation for a handful of guidelines and understandings for engagement that the two of you discuss and agree upon when times are simple and sweet.

- We all have a primal need to feel safe and secure; we have a deep need to love and feel loved. Establishing a process can help us meet our relationship goals more often than not.

- The process can take the zap out of a relationship; it's our own personal relationship lightning rod. Thanks Ben!

- True change comes from within. If you want to create lasting change in your relationships, start by examining your own behaviors and needs.

Inspired Actions

1. One of my favorite things to do early on with individuals and couples is to ask them to describe, in writing, a typical dinnertime experience when they were 10 years old. It's a great exercise. It pushes people back to a particular time in life and helps highlight events that may have shaped them. It's not always one specific night they remember, but more of an amalgam of experiences.

For some, it's like dreaming into it. One client reported this response to a "typical dinner" at age ten:

Typically, mom was in the kitchen serving. Dad would come home and crack open a beer, and wouldn't really talk to us until it was time to eat. We always knew not to bother him because he was tired. Everyone has his or her own spiel. I always felt criticized. If I didn't have something important to share from school, I didn't feel valued or interesting, so in relationships I find that I am constantly trying to find something to say that is interesting or witty. Otherwise, I'm worried that my partner won't love me or be interested in me, and then they might leave.

The universe is made of stories, not of atoms.
—Muriel Rukeyser

Take a few moments and write down your snapshot of dinnertime at age ten. Things to consider include: who's present, what's the vibe, who's speaking the most, what's the topic of conversation (if there is one), what other things are happening in the environment (is the TV on, is the dog begging), etc. If you have the opportunity, ask your partner to read your story back to you out loud. How does it feel to hear your partner read your words out loud? Does anything in particular strike you when you consider the memory?

Doing this exercise identifies certain areas where we have both positive and negative memories and can build upon our last exercise of telling our seven-minute story. Sometimes the dinner snapshot fills in empty space that our life story might have missed. Do you notice anything about your story then and the story you've been telling yourself about your life now?

2. Keep a Platitude Journal. Divide the paper in half and on the left side write the negative, frustrating, irritating, crazy-making things that you feel about your partner. On the right side, list the qualities you truly appreciate and admire about your partner. These may even be elements of their personality that you've been missing lately but used to make you smile.

3. Reminder: If you haven't yet downloaded your Action Guide (See Appendix for link) take this opportunity to do it now so you can appreciate the full effect of the book!

Chapter Two

Tool 1: Uncovering the Self

> "Self-knowledge" means becoming conscious of the
> unconscious: facing our shadow and becoming aware
> of the reality of our "inner partner," the animus
> (for women) or the anima (for men).
>
> —C.G. Jung

By the time many couples find their way to relationship rehab, they're at the end of a whole lot of rope. There's typically a great deal of blame, hurt, sadness, and, oftentimes, a massive dose of confusion. Folks are also usually feeling pretty crispy from lots of zaps and minor pyrotechnics. Many people feel so incredibly stuck that staring into the vastness of the emotional rubble can feel as daunting as moving mountains.

The work involved in couples therapy is about getting unstuck from a place of fear, ignorance, and ambivalence. Often, the dance of negative cycles can spin a relationship into such a chaotic state that it seems irrevocable. And yet, what we're desperately shouting for is to love and be loved, to feel safe within the context of the relationship, and to feel that the majority of our core needs are being met more often than not.

I didn't stumble upon this notion by accident. In fact, it came quite literally as the result of a wacky experience I had in the desert. In my early twenties, I found myself a mentor who had been around the block more than a few times and offered to coach me on self-realization, consciousness, and being a force in my own life. I desperately longed to know myself and I wanted someone to show me the way. My cranky Vietnam vet left me in the middle of nowhere with a jug of warm water as he crooked his gnarled finger toward the horizon and told me to move a mountain off in the distance. Before I could ask for clarification or protest, he drove off in a cloud of dust.

Sitting in the desert, my mind raced with angry thoughts and questions about my teacher. What kind of loon leaves someone alone in the desert? Does he mean I have to literally move the mountain? Is this a metaphor? Do I need to move the mountain within? Or is he so nuts he thinks I have the ability to move mountains?

I felt sick to my stomach. The thoughts looped repeatedly in mind. "I'm in trouble. I need help. I need information. I need someone to do this for me." Have you ever felt like this in your life? In your relationship, perhaps?

It was there, surrounded by sands and tumbleweeds, that I learned the foundation of my belief system: that, when it comes to relationships, we project excuses and obstacles onto others, both animate and inanimate. In that moment, I hated that guy. I thought he was nuts and was trying to kill me or make me as nuts as he was. But, that day transformed my perception of myself in relation to others. Being stuck in the anger, frustration, and fear I was projecting onto him was getting me nowhere fast. He'd already left the scene, what was the point? So I did the next best thing.

I started to focus on the mountain on the horizon and, suddenly, well it might have been hours, I guess, I had a moment of clarity. I realized I was directing all of my thoughts and feelings "out there." Once I had that breakthrough, I was able to go *inside* and move the mountain that was in my way. In fact, the only mountain in my life was the one inside. It was the bridge to awakening the way I have come to understand relationships.

I call this process of uncovering the self "Moving Mountains." It allows maximum growth for individuals within the context of relationship. In a sense, every relationship can be its own workshop for an individual to expand.

Even though the primary focus in my work is relationship coaching and consultation, my approach is primarily about individual responsibility and individual process. If you want your relationship to work, your relationship to anything or anybody, you're going to have to work on yourself first. The second that you depart from waiting on your partner, waiting for your job, or waiting for the government to change, the easier and more fluid your process of change, transformation, and illumination will be.

When you help yourself, you help your relationships. Taking personal accountability for your own joy and wellbeing is similar to staring at the mountain within, rather than seeing every anthill, every pile of garbage, snow, paperwork, or dog doo as a mountain.

How do you do this? Well, for starters you contemplate your own individual self as separate from your partner. Sometimes we must create some emotional distance from our partners in order to regain our sense of who we were when we started this wacky relationship. It may sound counterintuitive, but, in this state, we're ripe for a little old-fashioned individuation. The goal here is to understand who we are and what our expectations are. Knowing this shows us who our partner is trying to relate to.

> Individuation is the fulfillment of the law of life,
> so to be individuated is to be quite naturally united
> with the laws of the universe. And the fulfillment is on
> the conscious level if it is a matter of the human
> individual; such consciousness accords naturally with
> the totality of nature. (C.G. Jung, 1976, 297).

We occasionally throw around some heavy terminology in my field- big words for very big thoughts, ideas, and dilemmas. Some of these big words mean very little to me while others feel immense. Individuation is one such word. It's huge— because we are.

Jung clarified this concept in 1921. In general, individuation is the process by which individual beings are formed and differentiated; in particular, it's the development of the psychological individual as a being distinct from the general, collective human community. Individuation, therefore, is a process of differentiation, having for its goal the development of the individual personality.

Makes perfect sense, right? Well, I've been wrestling with this idea since I was a teenager. The concept that at some point in our development it becomes necessary to experience ourselves as some sort of Other seems at first to be a cruel reminder of puberty and middle school all over again.

We oftentimes confuse the idea of alone with lonely, but this isn't the case. Being comfortable by myself, doing my own thing, in my own way, is gold. When we individuate we become whole. In a sense, we become indivisible, meaning, it's very challenging to split off into fragmented parts or simply hide in the larger personalities of our parents or partners. The process of individuation is all about realizing ourselves as unique, beautiful, powerful beings distinct from others while still remaining connected with them at the same time.

Dr. Sue Johnson, one of the preeminent teachers of Attachment Theory in the context of healthy relationships, likes to distinguish the process of individuating *from* vs. the process of individuating *with*. We're all in a process of becoming whole, yet we do this in the context of relationships with others, not as a way to escape the very relationships that have helped shape us. Jung agreed on this point when he reiterated that, "if we stay on the path, stick with the work, we come to enjoy a widened circle of consciousness. Our sense of separateness ends and we gain broader, more intense relationships with others."

OK, let's say you get some space and feel more yourself. It doesn't mean the problems have gone away, I get that. The fighting and the distance and the bickering continue even if you know yourself a little better.

"It's not the problems, it's the process," I say to people every day. Every relationship has problems, but that's not what makes or breaks a relationship- it's the *process* by which we go about dealing with our problems that either works for us or against us.

Our job is to cast a new paradigm that allows dynamic, creative tension pointed towards a *way of being* in the relationship that exists outside of the issues and bring these challenges out into the open for resolution. It's essential that you reflect yourself, your thoughts and actions, back to you. In a clean, mindful, and compassionate manner, you must see more clearly your own reactivity and unconscious behaviors while potentially making incremental changes to the way you react, as opposed to respond, to your interior and exterior landscapes.

In this way, how you interpret and process the experiences of your life helps you organize the world into your own unique system and gives the relationships you engage in a real chance at thriving, not simply surviving. It's your perception of the world, i.e. whether it's friendly or unfriendly, inherently safe or dangerous, that's at the core of how you interact with that world. A good partner (or even a therapist or coach) has the special job of reflecting back to you these patterns of interaction and helps you reconsider those reactions that create pain or a sense of dysfunction. This is definitely one of the greatest gifts of being in a loving partnership — you get the benefit of seeing yourself reflected in the eyes of someone who cares. It's just not a substitute for doing your own self-reflection and deep inner work.

At its core, the foundation for this work is one of ideology and paradigm. Part of this process involves making a shift in your paradigm. When I speak about paradigm shift, I'm focusing primarily on the difference between a "transactional" paradigm and a "process" paradigm, which we'll cover more in depth in the next chapter. We're essentially looking at a fundamental shift from "this or that" to "this AND that." If you don't know who you are, how can you know what you want? Thus, I begin all couples work with each individual asking a series of internal questions which, if you'll notice, has *nothing* to do with the other partner:

Am I willing to do my own work?

Who am I, and where am I in my life?

What do I really want?

Where am I going and why?

Often, people become engaged in a relationship and make assumptions as to what the relationship is supposed to be, rather than what the relationship is. They don't always consider what they really need or want in their lives. Have you ever considered the reason you are in relationship? You know, what's the point? What do you see as the goal of relationships in general? If the answer to that is, "I want someone to take out the garbage," then you're starting from a premise of expectation that's going to inevitably lead to great disappointment. Your partner will never meet your expectations.

A part of getting to this kind of clarity is to question why love exists in our lives to begin with. Is love the same as a relationship? Is relationship success a birthright, a given? It doesn't appear to be, any more than having a perfect or optimal physical body is a given. I wish it were as simple as just claiming my perfect body and having it appear. But no, I have to eat right, exercise, sleep, drink water, and on and on. I have to take the raw materials and do something very specific in order to manifest the optimal body.

So it is with love. Love is the raw material that is simply handed to us. Sadly, it's not the case that optimal relationships just happen once love enters your life. No, you have to work on it, shape it, refine and organize it- and then hope that your partner is doing the same thing on their end. Thus, it's crucial to humbly accept that, while love is a gift, you are a mere steward of the gift. Nowhere is it written that you have the deed for life. You have to do the work in order to renew your contract and continue to refine, strengthen, and revitalize the structure that keeps the gift.

Not having a process, a consistent process, makes this kind of inquiry challenging. It creates chaos for many couples because people get stuck in old behaviors. We piece together scraps from the way we've seen interactions and communication done in the media, movies, books, and even between our parents. This combination is sometimes a catastrophe because it's based partly in fantasy. Sometimes the process we advocate for in a relationship is nothing more than a projection of what should be, rather than what truly is.

What's compelling about the type of paradigm and process in your relationship as a path to self-realization and personal happiness? Everything. Remember why our seven tools are so simple and yet serve as the best hack into the backdoor of Central Defense Mechanism Command?

This approach to relationships can set your coupledom on the right road. It will help you learn how to be vulnerable with each other and choose to connect in ways to make each other better humans. It will give you the opportunity to thrive, grow, and expand your own belief as to what happiness and peace are truly about. It will also help you find the truth of the love that exists between you and your partner. It's this space between the two of you that makes all of your hard work worth the trouble. Still, you can't consistently access that delightful place without trusting that the force field is up and running and will withstand most direct hits. It's hard to forget how wonderful your partner is when you are tearing them apart for things that happened years ago. Why are you doing that, again? Don't answer, I already know.

In order to get past the incredibly useful survival mechanisms that populate your mammalian brain (yet do your basic romantic partnership so much damage) you have to be willing to stand in your own marvelous radiance. If you can't stand in your own light, it makes it very difficult for your partner to meet you at the intersection where your greatness meets theirs. What's more, the Franklin Rod of healthy, conscious process must be firmly planted to harmlessly discharge your attacks as well as those of your partner. Operating under the assumption that since you have a great relationship and both clearly love one another, you don't require a system in place to deflect the toxic moments that can derail your bliss is not just silly, but borders on delusional. On the other hand, when you see yourself ripping into your partner, the one you adored just hours ago, you might need a little self love to make that medicine go down.

Tara Brach, in her book *Radical Acceptance* states, "(F)or many of us, feelings of deficiency are right around the corner. It doesn't take much — just hearing of someone else's accomplishments, being criticized, getting into an argument, making a mistake at work — to make us feel that we are not okay. Beginning to understand how our lives have become ensnared in this trance of unworthiness is our first step toward reconnecting with who we really are and what it means to live fully." Relationships are about playing the long game. They're about mastering the "art of more" in your life without fighting because you don't have what you want or running away to find it somewhere else. The answer is already in the space between you and your partner.

While Carl Jung mostly taught about how our lives are influenced by forces larger than we think, he also offered us some important concepts when it comes to the dynamic between partners and their connectedness to the rest of humanity. He spoke passionately about the *Conjunctio*, a marriage of sorts (even though it sounds more like a result of poor hygiene), between two people, two lovers, between the sacred feminine and sacred masculine. In order to experience this meeting between one's Self and something bigger, deeper, and wiser, a certain awareness is required.

Being fully aware, really present, allows you to experience the difference between yourself and that "something else." It also gives you the opportunity to have a unique, personal interpretation of that experience. You have to be committed to understanding and getting to know aspects of your own sense of consciousness, which you experience in various ways: the voice in your head, the unique way you feel about things in your life, and the way you personally experience your heart loving someone. This then gives you the opportunity to know the difference between what you know to be true in the world and what someone else knows or feels. Although we may have similar ways of relating to the world, your unique version or texture of understanding will never be the same as someone else's. Isn't that delightful?

Conjunctio is a love story. It is the meeting of two parts at some intersecting point where everything that is, was, and will be, come together and come apart. It is the place where *I experience you experiencing me* and it is my consciousness that allows me to register the moment, hopefully using it to grow and connect with myself.

In any kind of relationship, when people work on themselves, invest in their own growth, in their own deep satisfaction, the relationship inevitably transforms. All it takes is for you to respond instead of react in order to make that crucial change occur in your relational matrix because you are 50% of the relationship. As you change, your partner is going to have less to react to once you stop reacting to your beloved.

You now know the first tool from our Moving Mountains story. Awareness about Projection is one of the greatest foundations for all the other tools. As we move together in this space we've begun to create, we're going to need some additional tools to function properly in this change of paradigm. You will find that the way you used to communicate and work things out in the Transactional Paradigm just doesn't seem to hold much water in the world of Process.

Remember, Superman had no super abilities on his own planet. It was only when he changed paradigms and came to Earth that he found he could act in an extraordinary manner. The old ways of relating to one another will soon come to feel like Kryptonite — your energy will feel depleted, leaving you frustrated when you fall back on those default behaviors.

While we oftentimes wish we could just whip out a magical tablet (or a hammer) that makes our interactions more successful with our partner, the truth is that in this dimension, our greatest utility stems from our shift in consciousness and the lens through which we view things. Still, these ideas will come to be appreciated as if they were concrete, tactile implements to be wielded and used to build what we desire.

Renew Your Wows

- Don't just stare off at the distance at the mountains in your way. Remember, the most important mountains blocking your way are the ones within.
- Contemplate your own individual self as separate from your partner. You're a beautiful, distinct being with your own thoughts, feelings, needs, and desires.
- Every relationship has problems, but that's not what makes or breaks a relationship- it's the *process* by which we go about dealing with our problems that either works for us or against us.
- Love is just an ingredient. You are the baker who can turn it into a delectable relationship.

- To attain *conjunctio,* that amazing meeting point of two parts, you must first focus on your Self. This will allow you to better understand and experience your relationship.

Inspired Actions

It's important to make a distinction between knowing the Self and uncovering the beauty and brawn of the Self. We don't want to go so far as to lose ourselves in the notion that we're too good for our partners. I like to think of ego as: E.G.O. = Eliminating Great Opportunities. When the ego becomes too bloated and distorted you tend to push away the best chances you have at really establishing a positive working relationship with yourself. The opportunities are endless when you maintain a healthy understanding and appreciation for who you are and still humbly accept the places you must grow.

These exercises will help safely uncover who you are and not tip too far to either side.

1. Meditate. Mindfulness Based Stress Reduction (MBSR) is a fancy new science popping up everywhere from hospitals to boardrooms and it is largely all about meditating ourselves into a state of peace and acceptance. So, do like the CEOs do:

Sit in a quiet place with your eyes closed and your tongue resting on the roof of your mouth. Breathe slowly as you allow your thoughts to filter in and out. Repeat. (No, really, do it again.) Five minutes at a time for the first couple of weeks, then bring it to 10 minutes. This will not only serve to relax and clear your head, it will allow also you to de-clutter the static that has been hiding your essence from you and allow you more access to some of your greatness.

2. Journal. I know, who uses a pen anymore? Do it. Get one of those old fashioned notebooks and a nice pen and write at least a paragraph each morning or at night before bed. Why?

Because the more you get to know yourself, the more you know yourself. It's that simple.

3. Drop Down Moments (DDMs). Every time you think of it, take a deep breath and drop down into the center of your being and relax into clarity. Every time you feel frustrated, agitated, angry, sad or even numbed out, grab a DDM. Think of it as a random act of mindfulness, a shot in the dark, a kick in the crevasse.

4. Move Your Mountains. You read my story, and I guarantee that you have your own mountain range of seemingly impassable obstacles, whether they're in the form of a job, family member, partner, deep-seated feelings of doubt or low self-esteem, along with plenty of smaller peaks and hills.

Take a sheet of paper and draw a line down the middle. On the left side, write down a list of all of the mountains in your life, physical, relational, and emotional, even monetary. Next, on the right side, write down as many of the emotions you feel about each mountain and include messages you tell yourself about each. For example, a person I worked with recently stated one of their mountains as follows: "I have been working at this job for three years and while I like the work, my wife is frustrated that I don't get any raises and that I don't ask my boss for one." On the right side of his sheet he wrote: "I feel frustrated, angry, resentful, sad, insignificant, feeble, not good enough, inept, numb." He added: "Some messages I tell myself are that I'll never be good enough for my wife, that it's not ok to enjoy my work as it is, and that I'm a shitty provider."

When it came to process this particular mountain, this man was able to state the perceived obstacle to his wife and immediately list the feelings he had when he considers the obstacle. He was also in a position to share the voices in his head and the beliefs he struggled with about himself as a result of this mountain. Because he was able to communicate the entire package in a framework of self-exploration, his wife had a difficult time reacting negatively to him and was able to switch from defensiveness to compassion. She reached for him and told him she was sorry he felt this way and that she was grateful he could tell her in such a clear manner that wasn't about attacking her. As part of my work with him, we focused on where these thoughts, feelings, and limiting beliefs stemmed from in his life.

The crucial step in the process is to turn the mountain back to yourself and explore the part of you that keeps piling debris on top of the hill until it becomes a peak, and eventually, a full blown mountain. We are tremendously powerful creators and capable of turning molehills into mountains. We can also take them apart.

Chapter Three

Tool 2: Where Do I Live?
Paradigm GPS

> Loneliness does not come from having no people about one, but from being unable to communicate the things that seem important to oneself, or from holding certain views which others find inadmissible...The Pendulum of the mind oscillates between sense and nonsense, not between right and wrong.
>
> —C.G. Jung

Generally speaking, people treat relationships like one of America's other favorite pastimes — baseball. Home runs, winning, and losing are all hallmarks of our competitive spirit. As mentioned in the last chapter, we often wish we could just hit it out of the park every time and when we don't, we occasionally want to take the bat and break the ballpark.

Unfortunately, that "transactional vibe" doesn't translate well into a loving partnership. Many people believe that unless they're "winning" in the relationship, they are losing and all bets are off with regard to doing whatever it takes to prevail. To them, winning means running the agenda or running the show. While this sort of partner is looking for the homerun each time at bat, it's still true that they can wonder about, even worry, if their partner's needs are getting met while they, themselves, are left wanting more. They're not sure they can exist in a relationship where it's not always about them, or what to do when the other person has a need to be right as well. However, it's that inkling of awareness when they grip the bat and anticipate the next pitch that is most crucial to the movement of creating healthy process.

Contrary to popular opinion, it's not just men who think this way. While there used to be a wider gap between the sexes, there are many women who come from this orientation today as more and more women dance in the capitalistic model of transaction. As a result, traditional male and female actions and roles continue to merge. It's not as easy to discern who originated from Mars or Venus. We're living in a galactic melting pot.

Having said that, I find it is more often the masculine dominant partner who is stuck in a competitive model. I have to encourage people all of the time that just because they say, "I'm really sorry that you're hurting," or "I'm sorry you're frustrated or not getting what you need," it doesn't mean they're giving in or losing. It also doesn't necessarily mean that the apology holds any weight for the other. Asking for forgiveness or expressing deep regret is only truly meaningful when it is heartfelt and when the person expressing the sentiment stands and speaks from within him or herself. It means that he or she is being a loving partner.

For some, taking the love that is felt and experienced within the relationship is converted into the safety and structure of marriage. Marriage is an artificial structure you can create with a partner, yet it is crucial to remember that artificial structures are exactly that — artificial. If you want to lean into something that offers true assurance, lean into the magical space between you. It transcends the construct or format of your relationship, whether it is traditional monogamy, polyamory, straight, gay, transgender, kinky, etc.

When we create *in the between*, in the *sacred* space, it's magic, but it's not the marriage bubble that's doing it, or keeping it safe. It's the ability to be in the present moment, present *in the between*. When you create from that, it's not about being together no matter what. It's not about expecting anything.

If I'm expecting a behavior that I want from you, then I'm not being present in the moment, *because being present in the moment shared between us allows for this unknown to exist.* There is a creative generation of things between us that we just can't control. It's something that just is. The only thing we can truly offer is our openness and vulnerability, however raw or exposed we might feel.

Many people ask: "Can you get this out of me? Can you change my behavior? Can you make me into a better person? How long to fix this, Doc?" The answer is no, I can't. I don't believe in this kind of surgery. The day I started analysis, I asked my analyst that classic question: "How long is this going to take?" He said, "I don't know, are you a water heater? You're not a machine, I can't tell you how long it's going to take." You can't surgically remove a bad pattern and we won't be building Rome in a day. The best we can do is become conscious of our needs and behaviors so we can act with intention in the way we want to be. Here, the process can help us identify when we're reacting and when we're responding.

The life which is unexamined is not worth living.

—Socrates

Awareness: The First Step

When I speak to people about self-awareness, the first thing I tell them is that I don't want them to do anything different. I want them to observe. I want them to notice those moments when they react, and those moments when they respond.

The key to real transformation is awareness. When you simply notice, you are offering more and more awareness to yourself. In the beginning, the idea is to focus on simply observing and raising your awareness in small ways. For example, notice how often you react, even if it's hours or days after the fact. Check in with yourself and ask yourself, "Was I mindful when I did that or did it just happen?" If you can, count how many times it "just happened" and you weren't conscious. The more we start to take responsibility for our reactions and own them, the better we are at changing them.

When I began this work myself, I spent six months doing what I called *remembering myself*. I wrote the word "remember" everywhere. I printed it out and put it on my mirror, car, and books, so that everywhere I went I had this reminder to remember. Remembering is the same concept as "noticing," it's raising your awareness to remember yourself. There is a sense of accountability when you choose to remain awake to your thoughts, feelings and actions.

When you're noticing or remembering yourself, ask:

Who am I?

Who is it that is reading this?

Who is it that is thinking this?

Who is being present right now?

The same applies for relationship:

Who is it that's in this relationship?

Who am I?

Who do I want to be?

What am I doing about it?

To illustrate, let's say you walk into the kitchen and you're happy to see your spouse. The first comment to you is: "Seriously? You didn't have time to take out the trash?" Who do you want to be right now? There may be an impulsive part of you that wants to say, "go screw yourself," but who do you really want to be in general in your life? Do you want to be like Gandhi who is totally loving, present with yourself and with others, and only creates peace in the world? This is your chance to slow it down, analyze the situation in the span of a deep breath, and process the rules of engagement.

At such a moment, pause and check with yourself before doing anything. Your impulse is conditioned; your reaction is reflexive. Your reflex is to tell your partner to screw themselves, but is that who you want to be? Probably not. Who do you want to be? You likely want to be somebody who is accepting and loving and doesn't take everything personally. The fact that your partner is upset about the garbage really doesn't have anything to do with you. It has to do with their expectation and unmet needs. The question is, can you step into this moment with compassion and not react, but simply respond in a loving way?

You could respond in a way that aims to start a conversation about your partner's needs. For example: "It seems like you're upset. I'm sorry if there's anything I've done to upset you. Is there something that you need that you're not getting? Do you want to sit down and talk about what's not working here?"

Of course, you could also say, "Not a problem, let me take out the trash." If it's easy for you and you don't feel obligated, if it's a true gift and it doesn't really matter to you, then there's no reason not to.

Becoming aware to the present moment is about attention and focus. It's about rethinking paradigms and consciousness. It's about choice, intention, and motivation. What motivates me to change? I either want to be a better person or I don't. If my motivation is a desire to keep the other person in relationship with me, then eventually that's going to backfire on me. If I stop smoking because you don't like it when I smoke, eventually I'm going to resent you and take it out on you in other ways. Ultimately, it's about taking responsibility for our actions and decisions.

Many people believe that relationships run on a sort of transaction paradigm, which means that you're either right for me or you're wrong for me. You either love me or you don't love me. You give me what I want or you don't give me what I want. We ask questions to the effect of, "What's my return on investment in this relationship? Do I give more to you than I get from you?"

A transactional paradigm is what the business world runs on. In a transaction, there is an exchange of goods or services where the balance sheet changes. It's a win for one entity and a loss for another. There's a right way and a wrong way to look at something, a good deal or a bad deal. It's black and white, profit gain or profit loss.

As you can imagine, it's very easy to be frustrated, upset, and unhappy in a relationship where you're using the same paradigm that you would use to run a corporation. What's more, when we use a transactional model for a human relationship, both parties "lose" even though it may look different on a spreadsheet. Even when you think you won an argument or feel justified in behaving a certain way, the truth is that because someone had to "lose" in this paradigm, the winner can never fully rest knowing that whatever he or she fought for and won can easily be taken away. This is not a peaceful way to live.

But before you feel miserable that you're operating under these parameters in your own relationship, give yourself some compassion. Things don't need to be so grim. The good news is that you can change your paradigm faster than you can change the person sharing your bed right now. Change your paradigm and the world will instantly feel very different for you. This shift in context for your relationship will begin to remap the way you think and feel and interact with your partner because the map has changed.

Alternately, a *process* paradigm is about your experience– a felt, relational moment in time when all that you know is what you're feeling right here and now, even though that moment is usually experienced in relation with someone else. In this paradigm, you're learning, developing, and growing, all in the context of your emotions– or you're not. It's either what supports you, or what doesn't support you; where you feel present in yourself, or feel disconnected from yourself. It's a sense of feeling as to where you are in this moment in your life without comparing it to the last moment or a possible moment on the horizon. The only sense of success here is that both parties feel like they have been in dialogue together, they feel heard and acknowledged, and that there are no losers. In this paradigm, the currency of choice is emotion and it's exchanged through experience. In the land of Process our exchanges are largely conducted through meaningful interpersonal dialogue, appreciation and gratitude, as well as the ability to hold opposing forces like disparate thoughts and desires without exploding.

You want to move away from a transactional paradigm of "somebody wins, somebody loses, someone is right, someone is wrong." Those are the words of transactions, not relationships. Interestingly, as long as both partners operate from that paradigm, both will lose. Even if you give your partner what he or she wants, you may feel resentful and take it out on them later.

The best way I have found for relationships to work is to depart from the transaction mentality and move into a new paradigm of *process*. Instead of focusing on an outcome you want, learn to focus on the process. The process is always the most important component of keeping our interactions safe for both partners. For example, you may be really stuck in the outcome you want, such as "I want you to take out the garbage." However, process strays from having a specific outcome and lives in the space of dialogue and possibility. "How would you feel about taking out the garbage?" can be a game changer.

The metaphor I like to use for process is a steel pipe. There's something about a big steel pipe that feels impenetrable; something you can truly rely on regardless of the climate, the weather, or what's going on inside. Oil never gets stuck in those big pipelines stretched across vast expanses of territory. From a process point of view, it's something you can depend on. Whatever your problems are, the process will work for you if you're true to the verbalized tenets. If you agree to have rules of engagement with each other that you stick to and believe in and work from that place of process, then it's going to hold you and carry you through. Process focuses on the steel pipes, not where the pipes are coming from or going towards; Process serves a couple as essential infrastructure and provides a 24 hour support network.

In personal relationships, there can be issues that go unresolved for years. Having a process takes the sting out of not having an answer; it focuses on the relationship, not on the outcome. You have likely existed in your partnership without a "solution" to the big problems and perhaps there has been much suffering. Try this approach. There is no need to suffer.

> **There can be no knowledge without emotion. We may be aware of a truth, yet until we have felt its force, it is not ours. To the cognition of the brain must be added the experience of the soul.**
>
> — Arnold Bennett

When I ask couples, "What is the point of relationship?" they say very beautiful things like, "Sharing life with somebody, building trust, building memories, supporting each other..." While I love all of that, and it sounds great, the fact is we choose partners that push our buttons for a reason, even though we may not consciously be aware of that reason.

Sometimes I meet people who say, "We never fight, we never disagree, we never have a harsh word between each other." While that may seem wonderful, I'm usually suspicious because the more you really get in each other's lives, the more it's going to trigger different feelings and past patterns. While I'm not a fan of fighting and arguing, I am a fan of processing emotions and triggers and taking it as an opportunity for growth. On some level, we're giving ourselves an opportunity to be our best selves, yet being our best selves only matters in the big picture when there's an impact on others, like the earlier story about the Buddhist monk and the rickshaw driver. The monk and driver were actually engaged in an instant relationship, whether they were conscious of it or not. We all find ourselves in spontaneous relationships with thousands of perfect strangers in our lifetimes, from waiting in line at the bank, to sitting next to folks at a concert, to hanging flags on Independence Day with our neighbors. We always have a choice as to how we will show up.

Relationships can be one of the most selfish things we can do and I mean that in the most positive way. It isn't just good for you, it's good for all of us when you take the time and energy to create your best self. It isn't easy, but it's worth the hard work and effort.

In order to succeed in our desire to exist in a paradigm that doesn't measure success other than through our feelings and experience, we'll need a reliable new process that can ensure our positive experience. Keep in mind that process is about an agreed upon notion of how we choose to interact in order to live with mutual respect and understanding of ourselves and our partner. In the Process Paradigm, these established rules of engagement are the only structure that can exist in a world of experience that transcends value assignment. These tools are concepts that function as flexible containers for emotions and experiences.

Are You Ready?

You can read 50 self-help books and a plethora of relationship books and never know more about yourself in relationship than you will by actually being in one. Certainly they can be painfully challenging, making you wonder at times if you're just not meant to be part of a committed couple. But the truth is everybody deserves to experience relationships, and to enter into and exit relationships as needed. The only real challenge to whether you're ready for a relationship is your sense of self or lack of self-awareness. Deep within, you know the answer. To explore this, ask yourself the following questions:

- *Do I have as much to give as I feel I need to receive right now?*
- *Am I willing to be honest about it?*
- *What are my deep intentions?*
- *Am I willing to tell the truth about them?*

Oftentimes we forget that the people closest to us — our family, friends, and romantic partners — are experiencing the same objective events in their own subjective ways. In fact, it's a huge leap to assume they experience a cloudy day, an orgasm, or even afternoon hunger pangs in the same way you do. What does this mean? How is it relevant to feeling peaceful and connected in your life?

One of the crucial things to consider here is the notion that the way you perceive the "truth" may be entirely different from the way that it occurs to your partner. This isn't due to anything nefarious or malicious. Truth, as we perceive it, can be quite different for a multitude of reasons, starting with childhood development and experience, overall level of emotional awareness, spiritual consciousness, politics, worldview, etc. You and your partner were drawn to one another for exactly the same reasons you get irritated by one another, and this is exactly why you are different in enough ways to make things interesting!

I remember being in kindergarten out on the playground and being asked by a little boy and girl if I would be their priest and marry them. Without hesitation, I agreed to perform the ceremony under one condition: They would have to come to me for advice when they got mad at each other. Even at five years old I understood something truly innate, perhaps archetypal. True love is not immune from its time in the Soup. We all find ourselves, and our relationships, in difficult times regardless of how deep the love or strong the commitment. One of the very reasons I went into the field of psychology was because I have always been fascinated by the enigma of human relationships. Practicing in this field affords me the opportunity to constantly challenge myself about how I choose to relate in my own relationships. I constantly learn from the people I work with. We can all find more clarity in the collective consciousness through our struggles.

Just as sometimes we need more fiber in our diet, we need the stuff of relationships to do this. By composting past experiences, relationships, and emotions, we create the material from which we formulate new, hopefully more supportive, relationships in the future. Fiber is the metaphor for challenges, triggers, and emotional obstacles in life that create a chewing opportunity. It also does a lot to create a healthy gut, as opposed to white flour and sugar that goes down smooth. Similarly, milquetoast relationships do nothing for our personal growth and development.

When couples first come in for counseling, they immediately gain a different perspective of why they're in the relationship, a unique paradigm that they can dabble in and see if it's a fit for them. They get to try on a different way of being. If it works, it's a great short-term advantage or benefit in the sense that they've acknowledged to themselves that they're open to change and are embracing a particular path to that change. A long-term benefit is the actual change itself.

Have you ever been attached to this mantra: "I just don't know"? I've heard these words uttered by so many frustrated, lonely, angry people in relationships. It's amazing, really, to get to a place after feeling *so much* that we come to the little Island of Numb in the Sea of Swirling Emotions. We've been treading water for what seems like forever and it also seems like nothing will ever change. Will I just drown out here? Then it appears! Off in the distance, a tiny spec of green in the sea of blue— land! Only, when we finally wash up to it, we find there is only a tiny, tiny patch of land big enough to just sit and that's about it. Perfect, we tell ourselves, at least I can stop and rest. However, I've found that folks who find the Island of Numb oftentimes convince themselves it might as well be Club Med. They breathe deep, dig their fingernails in the sand, and prepare for the long haul.

"I don't know" is usually a cop out. We like to hide behind "I don't know" because it seems legitimate enough not to know and it serves almost like a Get Out of Jail Free card. "I don't know" becomes an anxiety meditation that can go on forever if we don't stop ourselves. I've seen couples who've been camped out on the Island of Numb for months and years but who pretend that things are really all right.

Do I like Who I'm Being Here?

> **Our deepest fear is not that we are inadequate. Our deepest fear is that we are powerful beyond measure. It is our light, not our darkness that frightens us most.**
>
> — Marianne Williamson

It's not unusual for one person in the couple to feel like, "How did I get here, is this what I want? We wake up each day and I wonder, is this what I really want? I hate the ocean, so why am I living on an island for my partner?"

It's a big question.

Most people enter a relationship with the misperception that, "If it's really right, and this is the right partner for me, then it should all click." They think if they find the right partner then they will never disagree, everything will make sense all of the time, and they won't have to put any work into it.

Nothing could be further from the truth.

I was sitting with a couple and the woman was crying. She kept saying to her partner, "Why can't you give me what I need? Why can't you just love me, nurture me, and ask about my life?" He just looked at her with this blank stare, and said, "I don't even know what the hell you're talking about. This doesn't register for me; I don't get it. Of course I love you, but

I don't know what you are talking about." He had no clue that what this woman wanted was a true connection. She told him, "I want you to care about me in a deeper way. I want to feel it in a deeper way."

How many times can a person say to someone, "Here is what I need" and not get it before they start to ask bigger questions such as, "Is this really the right partner for me, or am I just resolved to not having what I want?" When a relationship is not fulfilling needs, at some point people will ask themselves if this is what they want.

For example, say you're hypersexual, and have an intense libido. If you don't have sex three, four, five times a week, you feel frustrated. On the other hand, your partner grew up very religious and has a lot of hang-ups about the body, about sexuality being dirty or only for procreation. Because of this, you don't share the same libido and experience a great deal of resistance to sexuality. If your partner is not willing or interested in doing work on his or her sexuality, and you're constantly angry and resentful about not having the sex life that you thought you'd have, it's going to bring up larger questions and stronger emotions.

Do I deserve to have what I want? Why would I choose a partner that's not on the same page as me? Did I think I could fix them and make them come around to what I want? Will I ever have what I really want anyway? Am I with this person because I don't feel like I deserve more? I guess I can just be angry and resentful at them for not having the life that I want.

Part of the exploration is finding the line between going out and getting what you want versus saying "maybe I have an issue." It's a valid inquiry but not one that can be answered at first glance. I encourage people to immerse themselves in the Process for at least several months before they entertain the prospect again of making big decisions about their relationship. It takes about three months to establish a lasting foundation for a new paradigm and a new way of communication, so it's going to be at least six or seven weeks before we can even start asking the bigger questions about the relationship. Stop asking big questions for a while.

Take a vacation from figuring it all out. Focus on being present in the moment with yourself, your partner, and your new process.

The real work in relationships comes when you start to challenge each other's worldviews. It's more of those subtle nuances and interactions that push the less obvious buttons. In the beginning, the more common buttons are, "what side of the bed do you sleep on? How do you like your coffee? How are we going to deal with your parents?" Later, it becomes, "I don't feel like you hear me, I don't feel like you really want to meet my needs, I feel like you take me for granted." We begin to project deeper issues onto the other person. In order to truly renew your wows, you'll have to go back to the drawing board and create a new paradigm where you can both feel safe and that resonates for both of you. That's where change starts.

One of my greatest success stories was with a couple that had been married for 14 years. They had a very pleasant dynamic in dating, but had never really gotten over the hump of simple politeness - they just cruised into marriage and drifted apart. They had no idea how to communicate with each other. Eventually they stopped having sex, stopped communicating about anything meaningful, and started having emotional affairs with people at work. In essence, they stopped feeding their own relationship. All they did together was irritate each other and blame each other for things not working. A core problem was that their original purpose for being together was never consciously established. They had an attraction and that was it. The relationship had never developed in terms of a deeper connection; they never got into that place and had nothing to refer back to.

I went back to the beginning with this couple to rediscover, or newly uncover, the purpose of their life together. They had never taken the time and space to dream a dream together. They simply co-existed. In a series of sessions, each partner found a voice for their hopes and dreams, their fantasies about life together and even their sexuality. When you can fully accept responsibility for your needs and for what's taking place in the relationship, anything can change. This husband and wife found a path back to responsibility and away from the all too familiar state of blame. They decided to choose a new reality for their relationship contract.

If your paradigm shifts from one of blame to responsibility, would you think about your life differently? My answer is, "Of course." It's impossible to stay angry with your partner if you know it doesn't have anything to do with your partner.

These aspects of a paradigm shift can't happen overnight. I might make an intention to change, but a ship in motion takes a significant amount of time and energy to come to a full stop before it can redirect itself and focus its momentum in a different direction. That's how relationship patterns operate. They're like big cruise ships with lots of buffets and endless refills that require a clear process in order to switch course by a degree. In order for the luxury liner of your once perfect relationship to recalibrate and change course toward something more aligned with who you both are now, you're going to need some space to dream together. Imagination requires a suspension of reality or expectation that many of us adults have put on the shelf for any number of sad reasons. In order to see where the two of you have made your relational home without judgment or criticism, there will need to be a shift in the way you dream your life together. Imagination is fun, ask any kid. Intention is just the adult version of imagination and, therefore, can also be fun. So, it's time to imagine life together in a different place. Ready to have fun?

Renew Your Wows

- Gain awareness by observing. Don't change your behaviors, just note that they're happening and when they are happening.
- A transaction paradigm is one that is black and white, win or lose.

- A process paradigm is one that exists in the context of felt experience and takes place in this moment, in the here and now.
- Relating within a process paradigm takes away the notions of winning and losing and places the experience of loving and being loved in the present.

Inspired Actions

1. In order to establish a solid foundation for your renewal platform, the most important focus is paradigm awareness. You want to understand which paradigm you've been operating from and which paradigm feels like a good place to go. To understand this, explore these questions:

- What's your picture of what your relationship is for you?
- What's the difference between responding and reacting?

2. Atonement to Attunement Exercise: While we innately desire closeness, we oftentimes have a funny way of going about attaining it. This exercise will highlight the areas in your relationship that require a process of healing and forgiveness to clear the air for deep attunement with one another. Start by placing two pillows or cushions on the floor and sitting with your backs to one another.

Take a few moments to breathe deeply in silence and feel the rhythm of each other's breaths. When either of you feels ready, softly express with your eyes closed whatever comes to your mind that remains unresolved and that you might need closure and healing or forgiveness around. Whenever one of you expresses something that is still a raw spot, the other can softly respond with: I understand, it makes sense that you feel that way, I am sorry, please forgive me, or I want to feel close.

3. Read a book out loud together each night for a few minutes. Choose a book you both are interested in and take turns reading to one another for a month.

4. Name that Paradigm. Read and consider each of the following statements. Is it a Transaction paradigm or Process paradigm? Write down your answers.

- The universe is essentially an unfriendly place. We all have to constantly overcome the forces out to hurt us.
- The universe is conspiring in my favor right now.
- I am not only capable of making mistakes, but I often make sizeable mistakes.
- I believe that when it comes down to it, there is a right way and a wrong way and I must be on the right side of things.
- If I don't know what time it is, I begin to panic.
- Life is a process of whack-a-mole whereby I simply spend my time putting out fires and dealing with problems as they rise up out of the dust.
- Love is a verb. It is all about what we do with our feelings not what we say we do or don't say.
- Sex is like going to the gym more than it is a time to make love.
- Someone is always right in a situation and it is important to make sure they do not think they were right when they were clearly wrong.
- There is a hierarchy of needs in life so until I feel satisfied that my food, shelter, and retirement are taken care of, feelings will just have to wait.
- Relationship is a fluid, dynamic process that must be cared for in ways that go beyond structure and institution.
- If I'm bored or anxious in my relationship, there must be a problem that needs to be fixed.

5. Based on your answers in the previous exercise, you should have a pretty good idea as to what paradigm you gravitate towards. What's the difference? Nothing, really, unless your partner gravitates toward another paradigm. If that's the case, it's essential that the two of you discuss where your needs are being met and where you're missing the mark. It's quite

possible that the reason has a lot to do with a different orientation about the world, which is making it challenging to see the other's needs as primary. Here are ways to deal with this:

- Have a conversation about the way you both picture your relationship, your "coupleship," in the world.
- Dream together about the next two years:
  o Where do we see ourselves in two years?
  o How do we see ourselves getting there?
  o What are our primary goals vs. secondary goals?
  o If we had to visualize our relationship as a GPS program, how far apart do our little icons pop up?
  o Is there a great distance between our orientations, our goals, or our values?
  o How far before I arrive at my destination?
  o Is it *our* destination?

Chapter Four

Tool 3: (Be Response ABLE) Respond Instead of React

> Love doesn't just sit there, like a stone; it has to be made, like bread, remade all the time, made new.
>
> — Ursula K. LeGuin

A number of years ago my wife and I were audited by the IRS. If you've ever been through something like this, you know it's an incredibly stressful, upsetting, frightening experience. We'd been married only a couple of years at the time and had never faced anything so intense or threatening. It's a funny story now, though scary at the time. The government's computer somehow flagged us as potential international criminals and assigned the International Fraud Division to investigate us.

"Mr. Sumber, how do we know this therapy office isn't a front for a major transnational car smuggling ring?" Again, funny now- not so much then. In the moment, being grilled by good cop and bad cop in my office, on the same couch that would later be inhabited by happy wife and sad husband, was almost too much to handle.

One of the recurring fears I had during those many months was the thought of somehow being separated from my wife. It generated real panic for me, and also affirmed how much I wanted to be in my life with my partner. Sometimes, we're not so "lucky" as to be offered a threatening situation to make us appreciate what we have. Oftentimes, we must find the reasons to stay with our partner without feeling threatened.

We are regularly invited by life to ask, "who am I" and "what do I want?" We're called on a regular basis to check in with ourselves, not just our partners. Consider it personal responsibility to stay connected with your "why." Why be here? Why do I want to be with them? Once again, our process draws us back to our relationship to self and the deep work it requires to know who we are.

Part of knowing who you are is decoding what you're going through at any particular juncture of relational interaction. Is this about me or something else? Am I sure it isn't about me? Come on, is there nothing about me here? Why do I continually feel dissatisfied or numb or like leaving?

Are you willing to get off the break up train? It's very common to come to a point in our relationships when we feel *blah*. Perhaps there used to be consistent waves of excitement and passion, but now it feels like you're just hanging out, doing other things while you wait for a breath of fresh air to recapture your interest. Or, maybe you're at a point where you're waiting for them to do or say that thing that drives you nuts just one more time. It's extremely difficult to renew a relationship when you're in "one-shoe mode," meaning all it'll take is for one shoe to drop and you're gone.

Imagine walking into a bright, beautiful room and scanning the wall to either side searching for the Dark Switch. That doesn't make much sense, right? And yet, we tend to do the same thing in our relationships when we're feeling frustrated, physically distant, or emotionally detached. We look for the negatives rather than the positives. It becomes as automatic as searching for the light switch. You come to expect there to be points during the day when your partner blows you off or just generally irritates you. This is a great indication that no matter what you read or practice at home (or discuss in couples counseling), until you decide you're grateful for the opportunity to rally the relationship and see what can be created, you're bound to manifest more darkness.

One of my favorite symbols from twenty years of Jungian studies is that of the ouroboros, the serpent that eats its own tail. Symbolically, the reflex that so many of us experience where we "shoot ourselves in the foot" or "put our foot in our mouth" speaks to the human tendency toward self sabotage typical through cyclical behavior and redundant expectations. While we have a real pull to reproduce similar situations, including relationship patterns from the past, there's also a component of our cyclical nature that speaks to our inherent desire to renew ourselves. The end of things is often connected to the beginning of things, and so it is in our relational cycles. How we process a rough spot in our relationship impacts the way we turn it around. There is a level of wholeness and completeness when we process some of the old, stuck places in our relational dynamic through a new lens and use new responses that generate the kind of change that brings us deep satisfaction, a feeling of connectedness, and yes, a state of joy.

A useful exercise when we come to this place of negative anticipation and pre-blame is to take the notion of a gratitude journal in a slightly nuanced direction. When you feel yourself not only waiting for the other shoe to drop, but slyly nudging it closer to the edge with your pinky, it's time to keep a 30 day Platitude Journal. Typically, platitudes are overused, empty, trite comments we make when we're just so tired of everything and so devoid of sincerity that all we can muster is the same old cliché that makes people feel worse than if we'd said nothing at all.

The task at hand is to write a platitude in your journal each day that reflects a comment or belief you've been saying or feeling about your partner and then to write something that you actually appreciate about your partner on the other side that you truly do admire, like, or miss. Do this for thirty days. You'll begin to strip those platitudes of meaning and rediscover your partner.

The blame game is over. We're not going to spend any of our time, and our work, looking at the other person saying, "it's your fault." In order to have a real meaningful connection in any relationship, there has to be a give and take with vulnerability and trust. I can't trust you unless I feel that you're willing to be vulnerable with me, and vice versa. I can't expect you to really open up to me unless I'm real with you. And being real means I'm going to help myself when I'm feeling jealous, triggered, angry, left out, or unimportant. That's my responsibility because they're my feelings; they're about me.

The challenge many people have is in communicating what is true for them. They confuse what they're experiencing with "why you are doing this to me", so they don't take responsibility to be vulnerable and say, "this is about me, not you, even though I probably wouldn't be experiencing it if you weren't around."

The only premise for not taking responsibility is laziness and stubbornness. Refusing to take responsibility is refusing to come from a place of true connection or desire to create change. It's a cop-out, a justification for reacting instead of responding, for simply not feeling like doing it differently or willing to look at any other way of being.

Reactions versus Responses

If you think you're too small to have an impact, try going to bed with a mosquito in the room.

— Anita Roddick

Reactions are knee jerk actions based on a particular stimulus. According to science, we react to things all day long. We're reacting every second, whether cognitively or neurologically. The challenge is to accept that we're going to have those reactions and to take responsibility for them. Even though we have the impulse to react, we don't have to act on it. This kind of impulse to react comes from years of conditioning. It didn't happen overnight.

Nothing is involuntary, other than the impulse to react. We don't get rid of these impulses. *What we get rid of is the reflex to simply believe that I have no choice.* Notice I'm not saying I have a choice about the *impulse* to react. If someone steps on my foot, I feel the impulse to yell out in pain. However, I may decide not to yell if I'm in the middle of a symphony where there are tons of people who are silently listening to music. How do I not yell? *I respond and I choose to do it differently.* How do I do that? Because, in this second, I have weighed my options and I've decided that it's in my better interest not to scream out loud.

Some of our reactions are learned behaviors under specific conditions that began in early childhood. Since we were children, we've been trained to react in particular ways. If while driving on the highway, someone swerves into your lane and your father screams at him and gives him the finger, then that's typically going to be your conditioning. When you get older and start driving yourself, it's likely you're going to be impacted by having watched your parents' reactions. Chances are good you'll want to react the same way. That's conditioning.

Does this mean you should never get angry? Not at all. Anger is a perfectly healthy emotion to have, but we need to express it in ways that won't hurt others. There's a difference between people who use anger for control and manipulation in order to get what they want versus someone who's getting angry because their needs aren't being met. For many of us, anger is a secondary emotion, one that often comes too easily. It's generally not about what it is we're responding to, but a cover-up for emotions like sadness, hurt, anxiety, and fear. Anger twisted into a secondary emotion is just simpler. It's always on the tip of our tongue and fingertips. It's more acceptable for people to be angry than to display more vulnerable emotions.

In a healthy relationship we should always express anger when it's real for us. The challenge is, how do we express anger in a way that isn't harmful? The easiest, most honest way is to just say it–"I'm feeling really angry right now." That's it. Consider where your anger is coming from so that you can share the information you have and allow your partner to understand. You can say that you feel triggered, frustrated, resentful, or like you're not being understood — all of these are legitimate ways to express anger. You can tell them you're angry because you feel too much responsibility falls on your shoulders, or that you're feeling resentful but aren't quite sure why. The important thing is stating your emotions, rather than falling prey to reacting in ways that push our partners away.

If I start screaming and banging on the table, that sends the other person into a state of fear, putting them in a defensive mode. They stop listening. There's no excuse for raging at anybody. It's designed to intimidate and control. If I rage enough, I will basically scare you into submission temporarily and will regain control. This approach is another way to answer my own anxiety or fear of being out of control, but it won't solve the underlying issues.

When I speak about anger, in this context, I'm referring to when someone gets upset, not when they're exploding and causing fear for another person. For example, a man came in to see me and was constantly getting angry that his girlfriend didn't want to spend one-on-one time with him. Every time they went out it was with a group of people. He was constantly frustrated because he wanted more focused attention and to feel that she was devoted to him. She just wanted to go out to have fun and be social. He felt that he was just an afterthought to her, which left him feeling explosive resentment and anger. Sometimes it would come out in a scary rage, which would then push her away. It was at this point he came in to see if I could try to help him cover up his anger. Sort of like Western medicine, where we say, "can you give me an aspirin? I have a headache." Rather than, "why do I keep getting headaches?"

When he sat down, he asked, "Why do I even want to win someone over when they don't care about my needs to begin with? We don't seem to be on the same page." He longed for a deeper connection and focused, special attention. What he communicated was blame, criticism, and expectation. He clearly identified his transactional paradigm in his need to win her love or lose it. It was unlikely that he would ever get what he truly wanted using this approach. After some exploration, this man was finally willing to take responsibility for the way his mini tantrums kept his partner at bay and pushed her to prefer large groups because she didn't feel safe with him one on one.

Then he decided to respond instead of react. It was music to my ears when he recounted his brave new communication to his girlfriend: "I want a partner who wants to be close with me so that we can deepen our connection by spending special quality time together. I want to feel like I'm special and a priority for you, as well. I'm sorry I made you feel bad and wrong and got scary mad."

His girlfriend stared at him with eyes wide for a moment, tilted her head, and promptly began to sob. "I always wanted to be close but I never felt like I could do anything right for you, so I stopped trying. I felt terrible about myself," she told him.

While his behavior did indeed change within a couple of weeks, it took many more weeks for this man to unpack the reasons for his months and months of less-than-loving behavior as a means to get more love. He finally figured out that he carried a little mouse in his pocket that reminded him constantly that he didn't deserve to be loved. This little mouse assured him that his girlfriend's behavior simply proved the point. He was unlovable.

Many of us operate in our relationships with similar limiting beliefs. Do you really deserve what you want? Do you believe you're worthy of having a partner that is devoted to you? Is a relationship where people complain about their partners just how it is? Or are we hiding from the riskier, more vulnerable questions?

Everyone comes from a different premise in terms of why they do what they do, or why they don't do what they don't do. Many people say they just want to be happy. Yet, this is often an excuse for not going just one step deeper into the core of what we long for and why. We all just want to be happy, sure, but why do I feel I need to be adored so much? Why do I need to feel like I matter, or that I'm really, truly safe? It's just never that simple, is it?

We have a choice about whether, and how, we react or respond, no matter how long a pattern has been in our way. We don't have to keep repeating an action that isn't helpful or conducive to what we really want to create. Even when it's our first thought, we can stop it, although it may take some practice to take it off automatic pilot.

Reactionary behavior is catabolic as opposed to a response, which is anabolic. It's a huge difference. Anabolic energy is something that builds us up, like an anabolic steroid, also called "juicing." It builds muscle and it builds us up as emotional beings. Catabolic energy breaks us down. It's negative energy. It's something that takes away from us, makes us frustrated or angry. Because they're catabolic, reactions diminish us as the one reacting, *and* our partner, the one we are reacting towards. They also tend to lead to "reaction complexes."

Reaction complexes are when you react to something your partner did or said, and then they react to your reaction, and then you react back to their reaction, and then they react and you react, back and forth. It's a cycle of reactions that's a bit like watching a Ping-Pong match and it keeps a state of reactivity constantly in play. Typically we don't remember, or can't identify, what or whom started the reaction complex. We just know we can't get out of it.

Here's a common example of how this works. A woman comes home from work and sees the garbage overflowing in the kitchen. She gets angry and as soon as her partner walks in from the living room and with a weak smile says, "Is it so hard to take out the garbage?" Instead of, "Nice to see you, too, how was your day," her partner reacts angrily saying, "Is it too heavy for you to take out?" Then, she comes back with, "You know, I don't ask for very much around here, and I'm tired of being the only one who does anything." He says, "Well, I'm not the one making you stay. If you don't like it you can leave." She yells, "Well maybe I will!"

Sound familiar? That's a reaction complex. Who cares what we're arguing about? The question to ask is, is it really about the garbage? Of course not. It's about the way we're communicating with each other and the fact that neither partner is taking responsibility for the way we're speaking to each other and the way it's coming back.

On the other hand, a response is a mindful, planned action based on a particular stimulus that is weighed to a desired outcome. Responding doesn't mean that I'm not doing something. It's an absolute action. The question is, "Is my action going to work towards or against my ultimate goal of a loving relationship?" For example, if I want to discuss buying a house, I may ask myself the question, "is what I'm about to do or say going to create peace?" It may not lead to an answer as to whether we are going to buy a house or not, but if I speak about it in a loving, kind way, with curiosity and openness, it's going to create a space for response and openness.

Responses lead to conscious process where you're present in yourself and in the words that you're speaking. They're unique actions based on multiple factors in any situation. There's this moment in *The Terminator* when the viewer is inside the robot's head when somebody screams at him. A drop-down menu of possible responses pops up on the screen, allowing the Terminator to choose what he says. He ends up choosing "Fuck you, asshole" and appears content with his choice. Consider responding instead of reacting as making a conscious choice to select your response from your own drop-down menu of possibilities. There is no such thing as the "right" answer, only a choice we make among potential answers.

This type of paradigm shift from reaction to response, transaction to process, can be frightening for a number of people. If you truly shift toward a process model, you can not easily hide behind a transactional viewpoint that claims there's a right way and a wrong way to be in a relationship. In a process paradigm that is rooted in mindful, grounded responses, one is neither right or wrong and likewise there is no supposition that a ring on one's finger means you must behave a certain way. Process is an invitation to be authentic, present and kind. Plug that into your drop-down menu!

Renew Your Wows

- Part of knowing who you are is decoding what you're going through at any particular junction of relational interaction.
- Stop focusing on the negatives- until you decide you're grateful for the opportunity to rally the relationship and see what can be created, you're bound to manifest more of the same.
- Keeping a platitude journal can help you strip negative, clichéd thoughts of meaning, while instilling a new appreciation for your partner.
- Taking responsibility is an important step in enacting any type of change.
- A reaction is an ingrained, knee-jerk action, whereas a response is a thoughtful action that helps you achieve your aim of peace, happiness, or another goal. Responding mindfully is part of the process paradigm.

Inspired Actions

1. Take the next three days and change nothing about your behavior except paying more attention. Pay close attention and track the moments when you either see yourself acting in a reactive or responsive way or when you remember yourself having acted in a reactive or responsive way before. Pay close attention to the words you used, to the reactions or responses it elicited from others, and to the way it left you feeling.

2. After three days of step one, take the next four days and slow down your total response time so that you are able to breathe before every exchange you have with your partner. Ask yourself this question before you speak or act: "Is what I'm about to do or say going to create peace in my life?"

3. Catch the Tail Exercise. Take a few moments and write down at least three significant relationships, outside of your family, and what made them special. Next, explore these relationships and how they may have ended, if they have ended. Are there any similarities? Did you or they end things, or was it mutual? Was there anger or resentment at the end? Blame? Sadness? Did you jump quickly into a new relationship or take process time between? What have you learned from studying the ends and the beginnings?

Chapter Five

Tool 4: Thou Shalt Reject Projection and Assert Responsibility

> This is the real secret of life – to be completely
> engaged with what you are doing in the here and now.
> And instead of calling it work, realize it is play.
> — Alan W. Watts

Many couples have lost touch with the playful, easy connection that once made their togetherness so joyous and carefree. The idea that creativity and love exists in the bonds of relationship, in the mutual overlap between who your partner is and who you are, is tragically lost for too many couples. One of the things I hope to accomplish in my life and in my work with couples is to bring back that passionate spirit of relationship. The world becomes a better place when you rediscover the sweet spot in your relationship. Your neighbors notice, your friends and family raise eyebrows, and you quickly remember how much you'd missed the lightness in your step. So how did we ever allow ourselves to stray from one of the best natural drugs at our disposal?

Many people look at marriage as the end of life as they know it. And it is for many of us. If you commit to be in a long-term partnership with somebody, aspects of that old life are going to have to shift. However, the notion that you'll change or that you'll become somebody different from the person you used to be is not the downside, it's one of the best prizes! If done correctly, deep, long-term partnership forces people to consider who they are and who they want to be. Jack Nicholson, in the movie *As Good as it Gets* said it best: "You make me want to be a better man." Is that so bad?

Relationships provide opportunity in two directions: 1) You can use it to disappear *into yourself* or, 2) you can use it to appear in new ways, *to show up* in the world. I invite you to consider that really showing up, leaving behind the cave or the red tent, is the beginning of growing in ways you've never imagined. Things that typically help create trust in an intimate relationship include eye contact, body contact, a sense of comfort, ease in verbal dialogue, being fully held by another, and safety in silence. We all have things that help us feel safe. What makes you feel safe?

The challenge for any relationship, married or living together, straight or gay, poly or mono, is how to integrate communication, intimacy, and eroticism within the context of a healthy attachment matrix. Our sexual voices must be combined and harmonized in the melody of intimacy so that we're both happy, content, and safe the vast majority of the time.

In order for you to show up and feel safe in relationship, safe enough to dream it anew, you need to trust that who you are is secure and that your essence is not in question. Only from this place can you move into the conversation of a new paradigm and a process of interactive dialogue that supports mutual connection in its purest form.

In 1923, a brilliant, spiritually connected German philosopher named Martin Buber uncovered one of those obvious ways of understanding life that was hidden in plain sight. What he found had everything to do with the way humans relate and how the world is waiting for us to connect with one another in a meaningful way. His great work *I and Thou* paints a picture of the two types of relationship interactions humans tend to create. There are two primary relationships, one where I relate to you as a unique, self-contained, amazing *thou* and the other where I relate to you as an extension of my amazing *self*. As an *It*, you are simply here because I want you to be here and thus you're here to make me happy.

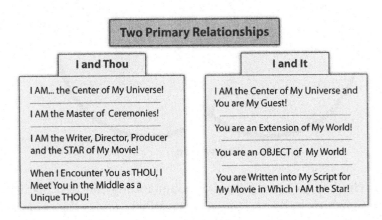

Two Primary Relationships

I and Thou

I AM... the Center of My Universe!

I AM the Master of Ceremonies!

I AM the Writer, Director, Producer and the STAR of My Movie!

When I Encounter You as THOU, I Meet You in the Middle as a Unique THOU!

I and It

I AM the Center of My Universe and You are My Guest!

You are an Extension of My World!

You are an OBJECT of My World!

You are Written into My Script for My Movie in Which I AM the Star!

Using Buber's paradigm of relating, we can see that there are two primary relationships we tend to oscillate between in close partnership. In the tension between the I-Thou constellation and the spin of the I-It, we learn how to meet in a place of mutual dialogue – in the space between. It is here that we're at the center of our universe, a place where we can be met and acknowledged as we are, a fertile presence of being and centeredness that our partner gets to see. It's like the Tao, the Yin and the Yang complementing each other's essence when we meet in harmony.

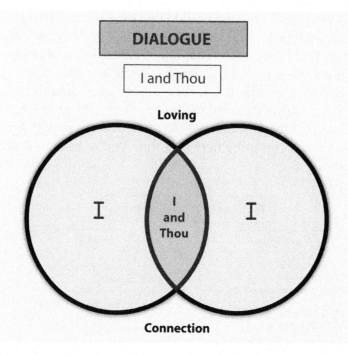

The key to *I* and *Thou* is understanding the two primary relationships in life: *I-Thou* and *I-It*. When you're the center of your universe as the writer, producer, and director of your movie, then you are at the center of your circle of life. If you're conscious and present, you encounter the "other" as a *Thou*, a unique Other who is likewise the writer, producer, director, and star of *their* movie. You meet each other at the center with humility and acceptance that you're both unique individuals having unique experiences. You meet in the *between*, in mutuality, and this space between you is where Creation/God/Creativity exists. This is where the magic happens. This is where you fall in love, where artists create art, and where you strive to exist on a daily basis.

On the other hand, the *I-It* relationship is when you, the star of your movie, as writer and director, move out of the *Thou* relationship and into a projection relationship where you confront your partner, not as a unique other, but as an extension of yourself. They're here because you're here. You, the writer, have written a part for them in your movie. It's as though you're saying, "I expect you to say the lines and act the way I intend you to. You're an extension of me and thus have no needs or individuality. When you don't meet my expectations in the *I-It* modality, I feel frustrated, resentful and consider writing you out of the script. I get angry and upset with you because you're here to make me happy, to reflect back to me my needs exactly."

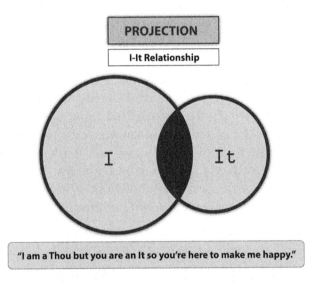

PROJECTION

I-It Relationship

I   It

"I am a Thou but you are an It so you're here to make me happy."

Not a pretty picture.

This concept has never been more important or relevant and I guarantee that you'll perceive your relationship differently when you view it through the framework of the two primary relationship experiences, Thou or It. For me, as well as for hundreds of my clients, this understanding forever altered life. It's virtually impossible to relate to your wife, husband, partner or friend, dog, or cat without somehow relying on this model if you want to really feel like you have a chance in the relationship game. It's a huge relief to find the once confusing interactions with your partner broken down into two simple categories: were we equals who understood each other and acted in a mutually respectful way or did one of us treat the other in a way that diminished their value or autonomy? That's it. All this philosophy and German headiness boiled down into the perfect filing system for your couple's needs!

If you accept that there's something more powerful than just you and your special friend hovering over your burrito bowls at Chipotle, then that's the space in which you can create the most profound connection you have ever known. Remember when I posed the enormously important question earlier about identifying who you are? There's a feeling we get when we're in a loving dance with someone that allows us to experience our own essence as part of the passionate shimmy. A creative explosion happens in the space between the two of you that can be used to heal and to shape your relationship through the mindful focus of your energies touching, whether it's the orgasm that you share with your lover, the moment of reunion when you pick them up at the airport, or the giggles that only the two of you can comprehend. And you, yourself and nobody but you, can experience this with complete wholeness. When things are in the zone with your partner you can say this and mean it:

> *I am at the center of my universe and you are the center of your universe, and together it's the two meeting in the middle... our overlapping space collapsing into one.*

You may recall the notion of *conjunctio* from earlier in our discussion regarding individuation. Remember, *conjunctio* is a love story. It's the meeting of both you and your partner at the crossroads where *I experience you experiencing me* and it is your consciousness that allows you to register the moment, hopefully using it to grow and connect with yourself. The space between two Thou's is one part of the magic we can use to learn more about ourselves and how it feels to be you in relation to others.

It's crucial to remember that it doesn't have to be tragic when a relationship ends, because all things in life come to an end. What's heartbreaking is when a relationship ends and there is an I-It dynamic in play instead of a prolonged I-Thou. When you and your partner both know yourselves and are in a place of self-love, then it is absolutely possible to relate to one another and see clearly from a place of mutual regard and respect if the union no longer serves you both. It's tragic when the narrative that we attach to makes the other person bad or wrong, or even at fault, and we distance ourselves from a place of self-awareness, and growth.

There's a beauty in death when we see the connection to life, even when it means ending a longstanding marriage or if it means moving out of your boyfriend or girlfriend's apartment after only six months living together. If you know yourself and who you are, then you know what you need and want; you know what you must do to create that. When both of you know who you are and what you want does not match up it can be an act of deep love and respect to amicably end the relationship.

Renew Your Wows

- There are two primary relationships, one where I relate to you as a unique, self-contained, amazing *thou* and the other where I relate to you as an extension, or off-shoot, of my amazing *self*. As an *It*, you are simply here because I want you to be here and thus you're here to make me happy.
- By recognizing our partners as a distinct Thou and treating them with respect, we can create a space for mutual dialogue that is loving and constructive.
- When we treat our partners as an It, we are stripping away their agency and making them a character actor in the movie of our life. Treating our partner like the amazing Thou they are empowers them to be the star of their own unique movie.

Inspired Actions

1. 7/24 Exercise: We all find ourselves in the Soup with our partners at some point. Hopefully, after a few chapters, you are feeling slightly less soupy than you did before. On the other hand, you will never completely eradicate the emotional soup from your diet.

The 7/24 Exercise is an encouragement to help you remember that your relationship is not all about the soup. When you find yourself in a rough patch with your partner it's important to honor the feelings you are having and not force yourself to do anything other than be in that experience, hopefully slightly more responsive than reactive.

Take out your calendar and swipe a week ahead from today. Highlight the entire day because in 7 days your commitment to this exercise is to devote a full 24 hours to celebrating, appreciating, and offering acts of kindness to your partner. Take the day and give with a full heart. Practice acts of loving-kindness. Text a love note. Email a favorite poem. Bring them a fancy coffee. Remind your partner that you care and that you are there. Feed the relationship.

This exercise will help you maintain perspective as well as stay vitally conscious that 7 days ago, you felt differently about your partner. Perhaps you felt you hated them or were so upset with them you didn't know if you could handle it. Now, a week later, you notice things aren't as intense. In fact, things are probably a lot calmer. If seven days actually, unfortunately, happens to land on a particularly soupy day, swipe another week and do it seven days from today.

2. Engage in a preliminary discussion about your "relationship process." Initiate a dialogue in which you

discuss the concept of emotional safety in your relationship and how, unless you both feel you can trust the other to adhere to certain guidelines, it might be difficult to open up and go deeper than the current spot.

Topics to discuss are:

- What makes me feel safe?
- What helps me communicate?
- What do I need in order to remember the tools and guidelines of the process?
- How often do I think we should be addressing the state of our relationship, and is that different from just living?

Chapter Six

Tool 5: The Check-in Dialogue

> **We could hardly wait to get up in the morning.**
> — Wilbur Wright

Benjamin Franklin was appointed to negotiate a trade agreement with France in 1776. He achieved all sorts of great political feats and he also enjoyed French women. A lot. Respected by politicians and scientists alike, Franklin was something of a romantic in his spare time. He was a great communicator, which made him irresistible to many influential French women. In fact, Franklin integrated his passions for peaceful dialogue and l'amour by actually spelling out his intentions and desires for various relationships with women. He infamously sent a "Treaty of Peace" to his beloved Madame Brillon which established clear needs and expectations so that neither party was ever in the dark about the stipulations of their relationship!

Our favorite Quaker (player) knew that dialogue is the key to mutual relationship, mutual respect, and mutual kindness. It's the thing that creates real communication with one another because it lives and breathes in the hallowed space between partners. When we consider communication, we should ask: Are we speaking *at* each other, *around* each other, or *through* each other, rather than *with* each other? A dialogue means that we meet in some shared, common ground and we dance a bit. Sometimes I lead, sometimes you lead, but it's a dance. It's not a power struggle or a manipulation of your will against mine. Healthy communication is never about a power play, yelling, or convincing.

I helped a couple recently where the husband said, "Of course I'm allowed to get angry, and I'm going to raise my voice from time to time, too." Perfectly reasonable, right? However, what happens when his anger becomes borderline abusive because he calls her names or slanders her character? What about the line that, if crossed, becomes raging *at* your partner rather than just expressing or communicating an emotion *with* your partner? If you're going to be angry, it doesn't mean you have to take it out on someone. You can feel the emotion of anger and still have respect for your partner. Mutual respect and appreciation for each other, and the process, allows harmony to take up residence.

Harmony doesn't mean always getting along, however. It simply says that even if we disagree, we know how to communicate with each other in a way that is respectful and loving. Just because we disagree about something doesn't mean either of us is wrong or one of us needs to be made right.

Process is what keeps harmony in the relationship because it allows people to meet in the space between, that "*I and Thou*" space where creation exists. Process is exactly what Ben Franklin utilized when he stated in black and white terms how his love affair would be conducted with a particular woman. There were understandings about the nature of their give and take, the level of monogamy between them, as well as the mutuality of their rules of engagement. The French loved Franklin's vision and expression for the American Dream as much as they appreciated his wonderful rod.

Remember, the goal is not to stay in *I-Thou* mode every moment. As humans, we're challenged to remain in that mutual dialogue constantly; however, the goal, as I see it, is to remain *conscious* of the dance between the two primary relationships, to be aware of myself slipping into an *I-It* projection, and to recover as quickly and as humbly as possible. The goal is to acknowledge my trigger to the other, to acknowledge that I am objectifying you, and to move toward a *Thou* space as mindfully as possible. When I react instead of respond, it's most likely that I'm unconsciously slipping into an *I-It* projection. We do this in every relationship, as friends, family, or lovers.

As couples full of love and acceptance, it's common to allow our partner to be and do what they will. This is typically more of the *I-Thou* space. Inevitably though, most likely when we're tired, hungry, cranky or otherwise triggered emotionally, we may slip into reaction and get resentful that our partner isn't doing, saying, or being something that we expect of them. For example:

"Wow, you're going to wear that tonight?"

"Seriously, you didn't unload the dishwasher and you've been home for three hours?"

"What's the point of being married if you're not going to take out the trash?"

"We haven't had sex in three weeks."

These are all *It* moments.

Thou moments are the clearly loving, mutually respectful situations. Making love in the purest sense is an *I-Thou* relationship because we allow for that magic to exist *in the between*, in the space of mutual divinity. *I-Thou* is patient, kind, and spacious. Here, we both respect each other in a mutual dialogue. The shared space is like a container in a good healthy relationship; both partners feed this vessel in their relationship. Healthy, mutually respectful partners go off on their individual journeys, live life fully and grow deeply which includes meaningful, powerful connections with other special people. It is essential to have clear boundaries with your partner as to what is accepted and what is not comfortable at the present moment. You take from your day all the deposits you've been making in yourself, and then you contribute to the vessel that you share between you. You continually build a stronger container for your experience and your growth together. For example:

"I appreciate that you folded my laundry! What an awesome surprise, thank you!"

"Honey, when you get a chance, can we talk about our summer plans so I can let my parents know if and when we'll be around?"

"How was your day? What went really well today for you at work?"

"I'm so proud of the way we handled things with our son today. We rock."

The Check-In

The purpose of the Check-In is to create an infrastructure for the process to work. We're creating that steel pipeline I spoke of earlier, for our communication to run through. Ben Franklin liked rods, I like pipes. Both work to keep your relationship safe.

The Check-In is a concrete, repetitive tool that creates change in the process for couples and eventually becomes integrated into the basic matrix of their interactions. The Check-In accepts that we move between *I-Thou* and *I-It* interchangeably. It's designed to raise our consciousness around those places where we're most susceptible, based on our unmet needs and projections, and in those places where our partners are perhaps stuck or more needy, thus susceptible to reactivity.

The idea behind the Check-In is that the more we practice it in the same way, sticking to its principles, the easier it becomes to enter a zone of safety and creativity. When we need to have a conversation that is somewhat challenging or emotionally charged, all we have to do is resort back to the structure of the Check-Ins. Consistent practice of the Check-in will help make it a natural way to communicate that you can utilize in difficult situations. The goal is to move from a place of conscious competence to a state of unconscious competence, where the behavior of the Check-In becomes so ingrained and integrated that you do it in your interactions without thinking about it. You'll be moving through an interaction with your partner one day and you'll come to the awareness that your ordinary interaction has actually been something rather extraordinary – you're allowing the triggers and the fight or flight mechanism to do its thing without feeding the inner animal! You're already safe and don't need to react to triggers or fear. The process between you and your partner will help to confirm this. This creates a structure for communication and leads to a truly harmonious, mutually respectful dialogue.

Dialogue isn't always about verbal communication. It's also honoring the energetic space between two beings. I encounter my partner as a beautiful being worthy of praise, acknowledgement, and affirmation, simply because. As one speaks, the other holds space and hears. Listening is not the same as hearing; listening implies understanding as well. So, receive your partner as who they are in the space between and hear them. As the recipient partner in the Check-In, don't respond to what your partner says verbally, simply witness and hold the space for you to be Thou.

Initially, the Check-In is a mechanical process: three things I appreciate, three things I need, and three things I'm willing to give in order to facilitate the process. When speaking, we face each other with full eye contact. We listen as the other speaks. We receive what's being offered. It feels mechanical at first, and it's supposed to be somewhat mechanical so that it becomes an automatic process. Trust the process. Integrate it, because it creates rules of engagement for people in relationships.

In the following chart, you can see that the Check-In dialogue revolves around the idea of appreciations, needs, and gifts.

Appreciations

Appreciation is the fluid that keeps the mechanism of any good relationship moving smoothly. It's basically the WD-40 that keeps your mechanics going. It's the machinery of any two people coming together. In order for it to move smoothly, general kindness and appreciation must be part of the process.

Sadly, some of us offer more kindness to strangers on the street than we do to our partner of 20 years. I find this idea tragic. By all means, be kind to strangers, but be kinder to the people you love. It's much easier to give an appreciation when you know somebody and it's essential to your relationship that you share even the tiniest acknowledgments you feel or become aware of on a daily basis with your partner.

Sometimes receiving compliments is a challenge for people. It's one of those things that vary for everybody. We all have our own issues. I might have an easier time receiving than giving, but it could be different for my partner. As a caretaker, I know it's far easier for me to give you an appreciation than to accept your appreciation of me.

One of the activities I have people do at my workshops is called *The Circle of Appreciation*. Participants begin by finding a partner and facing each other. They then take turns circling each other as they verbalize as many appreciations, affirmations, and compliments as they can think of in a couple of minutes. When time is up, they switch and find another partner.

It's amazing how many people aren't used to giving or receiving positive feedback of this nature. Given this, it's not surprising that once people get into a long-term commitment, they aren't conscious of how valuable it can be to the health of the relationship. Even when I have couples do this in my office, it can be challenging. In a couples therapy session, I like to have one person at a time stand with their eyes closed, and the other person slowly walk around them and offer every appreciation they can think of, lavishing them with praise and acknowledgement, until they can't think of any more. After both partners have done this, we discuss what it was like and where there was resistance.

It's hard at times for some people to accept all of the goodness that somebody reflects back to them. It can really push our buttons. For example, if I have body issues, which many of us have, and my partner says, "I love your body," I may go into a shutdown mode. I'm thinking, "This person doesn't know anything. I can't trust this because it's obviously not true." This common reaction reflects an issue with our sense of self as well as our inability to accept our partners from a place of Thou. Our partners may think of our bodies and talents differently than we think of them. Accepting our partners as a Thou also means accepting that the praise they offer, which may conflict with our own ideas of ourselves, is true for them.

Unfortunately, it's not just accepting praise that's difficult. Sometimes I get terrified looks from the partner who is supposed to be offering appreciations. It can take a little coaching if you're not used to expressing appreciation, even though it doesn't have to be monumental appreciation or super deep. It can be as simple as:

"You make the best coffee."

"Thank you so much for loving me."

"You are the best friend I could ever have."

"I love your eyes."

Another obstacle is when the person giving praise is resistant to doing so. It's the flip side of not being able to receive a compliment. People say things like, "I don't want this to go to your head. I feel like I give you plenty. This just feels like too much. I don't really know what to say. You know I care about you, and that's all there is. We aren't one of those touchy-feely relationships. Why are we doing this? This is stupid!" And on and on... This is generally a sign of other issues within the relationship. In these situations, I may ask the partner whose eyes are closed, "how does it feel when your partner has resistance to sharing what they appreciate about you," and a whole new dialogue opens up. Responses I've received include: "I feel terrible about it", "it makes me feel unloved", and "it makes me feel lonely".

Another thing to be aware of is whom you're actually focusing on. For example, when some people appreciate someone they'll twist their own ego into the middle of the appreciations, effectively making the praise about them. They'll say something like, "I appreciate that you have patience for me", "I appreciate that you like my sense of humor", or my favorite, "I really appreciate how you're finally showing up on time." Ouch. This is a spectacular way of talking about oneself and getting a little dig in there at the same time. It's important to recognize this behavior because it's indicative of an It mentality. Attention must then be paid to getting into a Thou state so that we can appreciate our partners as the magnificent Thous that they are.

Sure, you might feel self-conscious the first few times you attempt to offer appreciations. Yes, you might feel some resistance or anxiety from yourself or from your partner. Trust me, it gets easier. In the beginning, I encourage people to do this in their homes and practice, practice, practice. Become comfortable complimenting your partner for who they are and learn to accept the praise they offer you.

Needs and Expectations

Nothing is good or bad, but thinking makes it so.

—Shakespeare

In the course of working with couples, I often hear, "Oh, well, I'm not getting my needs met, so I'll leave." But it's never that simple. Are we being clear when we express our needs? Are our needs different from an expectation?

Many people act as if their partner should read their mind. When their partner doesn't automatically know what's needed, these people may think it's because their partner isn't "right" for them. Occasionally, this is true, but most of the time, it's not the case. More often, it's a communication problem. Unless I'm really willing to go out on a limb and be vulnerable and express what it is I need, then how can I expect to make a connection with my partner so they *choose* to meet my needs?

It's delusional to think that if my partner is right for me they will automatically meet my needs. Being aware of someone's needs happens over a period of time, it's not an immediate reaction. Your partner may love you, but still not know you in a long-term way. They may not always know what to do for you. A lot of people walk away early on in a relationship because someone isn't psychic. Wouldn't you rather be with a good listener that's motivated to please you, than be with a psychic?

We've had needs since birth, and, as children, most of us got used to having those needs met, especially the basic needs — food, water, and shelter. If we were lucky, we got positive affirmation from parents, family members, and teachers. If we were really lucky, we received hugs and physical affection. Generally speaking, children *expect* those needs to be met.

Then we grow up and go off into the world and individuate, separating from our parents. We have to find our own way, our own identity. More than likely, we'll have to go through a process of shifting from an expectation that our needs will be met to a communication of our needs and an openness to the response of our partner. *Most importantly, we have to take responsibility to meet our own needs rather than projecting them on to others.* The key to this is remembering that I am the only one responsible for meeting my needs. Don't forget the Moving Mountains story. While it's perfectly understandable that you'd like to project all of your fears and frustrations onto someone else, the only obstacles to getting what you want remain inside.

We're responsible for meeting our own needs. That responsibility is reflected in how we talk about our needs. The moment we communicate needs in the context of "you", and what "you" can do for me, we are off track. We get into trouble. The greatest way of communicating about my needs is to put me *in* to the communication. The best way to begin a statement about something I need is to lead with an introduction about feeling:

I need to feel loved.

I need to feel appreciated.

I need to feel I'm not alone.

I need to feel like I'm a priority.

I need to feel I have a partner.

I need to feel important.

I need to feel trusted.

These are affirmations of need. The difference is that some of us get off track by communicating our needs in terms of "*you*" and what "*you're*" going to do for me. For example:

I need you to appreciate me.

I need you to pay more attention to me.

I need you to act like a partner to me.

I need you to support me.

Why don't you love me?

When do you think you'll want to have sex with me?

This kind of language can automatically put someone in resistance mode. As soon as they feel like they *have* to do anything for you, it becomes an obligation and an expectation. They'll immediately start to imagine ways to *not* give you what you need or, if they are going to give you what you need, they do so with resentment. It's not necessarily a conscious thing, although, especially in relationships that are strained, it becomes more and more conscious.

The thing to remember about needs is that you're opening a door for your partner to give you a gift. *A gift is a present I place myself inside of.* I place my intention and my love inside the gift. You're setting them up for an assist. In essence you're saying, "yes, I can meet my own need, but I'm going to pass you the ball, and give you the shot – the opportunity – to meet that need for me as a gift to me."

There are different stages to this process. Initially it starts from a broad place of bigger themes such as "I need to feel loved." That's the beginning point of conversation. In time, my partner may say, "you keep saying you need to feel loved, I don't really know what that means. Can you help me understand what you need in order to feel loved?" When there's not a buy-in, though, it will only come across as an expectation. Expectations are a breakdown in the process, creating fracture and subtle resentment. I coach couples to never say, "I need you to do anything." Changing the language from *"I need you"* to *"I need"* can cause a dramatic shift in your conversations. Sometimes people get very flustered because they aren't sure how to phrase their need without making it about their partner, and that's the point. It's so ingrained that we must actively work on it.

The idea of this "needs" process is to open the door for my partner to become curious. Ideally it leads to curiosity, because if I'm with a person who doesn't care about, strive, or desire to meet my needs, I'm probably with the wrong person. You can't instill the desire to be truly interested in your partner. They either want to be there for you or they don't.

As you communicate your needs, express them in terms of yourself and who you are, independent of the relationship. Your needs truly precede and exist beyond who your partner is or the nature of your manifested relationship. The minute you express your needs in terms of *them* and what they are or are not doing for you, you free fall into projection, reaction, and the *I-It* extension of yourself and them. As long as you express your needs in terms of what you need them to do *for* you, you lose sight of yourself in your own life, as well as who you are – a being with inherent needs and wounds from birth on up.

You share your needs with a loving open partner because you want and need them to understand who you are as a loving, mutual witness to your journey. If you *expect* them to meet your needs, you will inevitably be disappointed and resentful. They might even meet your needs most of the time, but in those instances when they don't, you may feel wounded and hurt because you have come to expect them to take responsibility for things that you, and only you, can take full responsibility for.

When I communicate my needs as free standing islands of experience, the Who-I-Am-ness of me, I allow you to see me in my vulnerability, in the *Between*, in the Divine acknowledgment that I come with needs and wounds and hurts and that, more than anything, I want to love and be loved! Most importantly, by communicating my needs as something about me, it gives my partner the opportunity to grow more conscious of those needs, such that my partner is able and more willing to give gifts toward meeting those needs without the hook of expectation or obligation. But as long as I feel like I *have* to give you something, I won't want to and will perceive it as transactional. In other words, "I'll give you what you want if you give me what I want." That only leads to trouble.

Let me illustrate how this can work by sharing an example of something that happened between my wife and me:

When we started living together in the beginning of our relationship, the first couple of months were great. Then, at some point, my wife (then my girlfriend) started to have a reaction to the way I would come home from work. I would come home, kick my shoes off in the hallway, thumb through the mail, and leave it opened in the hallway. Then, I'd go into the kitchen, fix some cereal, leave the milk and cereal on the counter. I'd go into the office, check my e-mails and then leave the light on after I'd leave. I'd then move to the living room, turn on the TV, kick my feet up on the table, and start eating my cereal.

She'd come home and find my shoes strewn on the floor, the mail opened everywhere, the milk sitting on the counter, the lights on throughout the house, and me sitting watching TV without a care in the world.

In the beginning, she was really sweet about it, "honey, do you think you can put your shoes away? Make sure you keep things clean when you get home."

"Sure honey, no problem."

Then a month goes by.

"Honey, your shoes are in the hallway, make sure you put them in the closet."

"Oh yeah, sorry, I'll do that."

Another couple of months go by, "I can't believe you have so little respect for me and you don't put your things away. I've told you I need you to put your stuff away and keep things neat. You are totally disregarding my needs."

Another month goes by and it's "I don't think I can live with you, you don't care about my needs."

What was *she* missing this whole time? She made a good case. I loved her then and love her now. There is nothing I wouldn't do for her, so what was *I* missing?

I was missing a different way of communication from her that I needed in order to feel like it could be a gift I was giving to her in response to something she needed. What I kept hearing was that I was doing it wrong, that there is something bad about the way I do life. The message I heard internally was, "I'm a bad person and I need to change who I am in order to make you happy." So, of course, there was ongoing resistance to actually meeting her needs.

At some turning point, she finally broke down in tears, and gave me what I needed all along, which was the vulnerability, truth, and honesty about what she experiences when things aren't in their place.

She finally said, "I don't think you realize how important it is for me to have order in my life. Because when things aren't in order, I feel like I can't control my environment and I fall apart. I don't want to do anything. I don't want to work. I just want to lie on the couch and do nothing, and I feel terrible about myself. All these things that are out of place create anxiety for me."

My response was, "Why didn't you tell me all along!? How come you didn't tell me that?"

She looked at me like I was crazy and told me she had been telling me for six months. But for me, I couldn't hear it until I heard it wasn't about me. For the first time in six months, it was just about her: this is who I am, and this is what I need. As someone who adores her, that's all I needed in order to give her a gift of what she needed. This difference between needs and expectations is profound in a relationship.

Gifts

> **I have found that among its other benefits,**
> **giving liberates the soul of the giver.**
>
> —Maya Angelou

With a gift, you place yourself inside of what you're giving; however, it's not about ego. Offering yourself freely and completely as a natural extension of your love for another can be a purely selfless act, and, when received in that mindset, it can be tremendously healing.

If you notice that your partner has been on their feet all day, and they come home, kick their shoes off, and lay on the couch, a gift might be, "hey, can I give you a foot rub?" You're giving it because you see it's something your partner can benefit from and you want to do something for them. That's a gift.

On the other hand, a present is something you give without being inside of it, often as an obligation. A present is something that you feel like you have to give. It's conditional. If you go to a family holiday, like Christmas, and everyone gives you a present, what do you do? If you don't have anything planned and run down to Walgreens to buy gift cards to hand out, then those are presents because you felt obligated to give them.

The difference between a gift and a present is the motivation and intention behind it. Is my intention to shut you up so you stop begging me to be more thoughtful or is it authentic and mindful? Is my intention simply to love you for who you are?

Gifts can be tangible or intangible. For example, in the previous story of an early conversation between my wife and I, from a Check-In standpoint, she might have said to me, "I really appreciate that you've done an amazing job in your past living alone and thrived that way. However, I need to live in a home that feels safe and orderly so that I can reduce my anxiety. What I'm willing to do is sit down with you and explain this in very concrete terms so that you understand the ins and outs, of what works and what doesn't work for me, because I want to thrive together." In this communication, being willing to sit down with me and explain it all is a gift she's willing to give me.

Here's another example – one that I hear often in one form or another: A woman is constantly complaining to her partner that she doesn't participate in cleaning up the house after dinner. No one empties or fills the dishwasher and nobody takes the garbage out, therefore she feels like she's always the one in charge. She works, as well. After a long day, it's her job to cook dinner for everyone, and then clean up the kitchen while her wife relaxes on the couch.

What can I give to her as my partner? I could say, "You said you need to feel like you have a partner when it comes to managing the tasks of the house. You need to feel like you are respected and equal in the relationship. *The gift I want to give to you is I intend to be more aware of house tasks this week. My intention is to participate more when it comes to dishes after dinner.*"

Notice I'm being very careful to not be specific. I didn't say, "I will do the dishes every night this week", or "I will be in charge of emptying the dishwasher". Why? Because when you do say that, it's a setup for something to happen. Then, if you don't or can't follow through, you've disappointed your partner. Instead, speak from the place of intention – what you intend to do.

In Practice

The beauty of the Check-In process is that it can be used with couples for several other themed purposes. For example, a Financial Check-In. In this case, you would say three things you appreciate about your partner financially, three things you need when it comes to your finances, and three things you'd like to offer to support your financial health as a couple.

Or, it can also be done for a Sexual Check-In: Three things you appreciate about your partner sexually, three things you need when it comes to your sexuality, and three things you'd like to give (not numerically, but intentionally) to support them sexually.

To reiterate, if I'm doing the Check-In with you, then I give you three things I appreciate, three things I need, and three things I'm willing to give to you. The "3, 3, 3" is for practice purposes, to get the muscle moving for this communication. Down the road, it simply becomes integrated into the process of a relationship. It's something that we implement unconsciously, subconsciously. Couples attest to this years and years later that the Check-In just becomes a way they communicate.

Here's how an integrated check in dialogue flows between two people after months of doing regular, scheduled check-ins:

"So, I want to start by saying how much I love and appreciate you. You've been so good about taking out the garbage lately and I haven't noticed the toilet seat up once in the past two weeks. Something has been on my mind lately and it has to do with the garden. Every time I come home and I walk past the garden I feel really frustrated and triggered. We talked about it months ago and you agreed that you would clean out last year's dead plants and veggies. It has been a while and it still isn't done. I get that it isn't a particularly fun job and you might have felt like you had to say you would do it because I was upset when we talked. I'm at a point where I'm totally open to helping you do it so we can tackle what isn't fun together. Can we make it a couple's project? We could even go to that movie afterwards you've been wanting to see."

In this situation, the bones of the check-in are integrated into a brief conversation where the three components, appreciations, needs, and gifts, are all used as a way to express something that might otherwise turn into a rough discussion where one or both people feel blamed and criticized.

Renew Your Wows

- Dialogue is the key to mutual relationship, mutual respect, and mutual kindness.
- We can't always stay in the I-Thou mode. The goal is to be able to recognize when we've slipped into an I-It mentality and return to treating our partners as unique Thous.
- The Check-In is a tool which can help you communicate with your partner even during difficult conversations. When ingrained as part of your process, you'll be able to integrate the three steps to discuss anything from taking out the garbage to sex and financial matters.
  - o The Check-In follows this formula:
  - o Three things I appreciate
  - o Three things I need
  - o Three things I'm willing to give
- Appreciations are an important part of a relationship; in fact, they are the fluid that keeps the mechanism of relationship running smoothly. We often forget to tell our partners the things we like about them. Taking the time to compliment your partner and to share your appreciation is a way to show love.
- Needs are different than expectations. Needs should be focused on the self and not projected on our partners.

We are capable of meeting our own needs. When our partner chooses to meet a need for us, they're giving us an important gift.

- A gift is different from a present. Whereas a present can feel like an obligation, a gift is something you place yourself inside of; it is given without expectation and feels like a part of the giver is actually present.

Inspired Actions

1. Set up a day and time with your partner to do a Check In, giving yourselves at least 15-30 minutes of uninterrupted time. The day before, remind your partner about your date and give them the parameters so they can write down some notes beforehand. Allow each partner to offer their three responses at each tier before moving to the next. While one partner speaks, the other simply listens. No questions or comments are permitted until the entire process is complete and then only with permission. Permission is a show of respect and it's a very important rule of engagement.

2. Advanced Check-Ins. After you have successfully shared two months of check-ins, you are ready to move to the next level- utilizing the check in formula to have any challenging or triggering conversation that exists in your partnership. For example, couples I have worked with have done Money Check-ins, Co-parenting Check-ins, Intimacy Check-ins, etc. The key to remember in all of these advanced processes is that the formula is your friend and must not be pushed aside. Otherwise, you run the risk of easily stepping on a dragon tail. Sex and Money are typically two of the most charged topics for a married couple and care must be taken in order to ensure that the process of the check-in is your safety valve not the door that opens to your private hell.

3. Fire up the Chat Signal! Nothing fancy here — you don't have to break into Commissioner Gordon's office to do this one — just light a candle. One of the things I recommend to couples when they're formulating their process is to agree that either person can always just light a particular "candle on the mantle" when there is a sense that something is amiss in the relationship, when you are feeling distant, anxious,

curious, lonely, or even horny but you are feeling too nervous, shy, or even frustrated to formally initiate a conversation or facilitate the reconnection. When the candle is lit, both parties agree that they will reach out to the other and inquire as to what is going on. Perhaps it's time to schedule a check-in and the candle is a reminder to make sure it's put on the calendar. Perhaps I just wanted to connect and this gives us a chance to stop the busy day and hold hands for a moment. Or, perhaps it has been a while since we made love and I am lighting the Chat Signal to quietly initiate a higher level of intimacy. The candle on the mantle is a beacon of change. Use it!

Chapter Seven

Tool 6: Processing the Rules of Engagement

> **And the day came when the risk to remain tight in a bud was more painful than the risk it took to blossom.**
>
> — Anais Nin

Sir Isaac Newton, the seventeenth century natural philosopher, was indisputably a man of science. He laid the foundation for classical mechanics and modern calculus and famously formulated the laws of motion and gravity. He was a very heady dude by all accounts. One of the greatest gifts of his life's work had much to do with our topic, relationships. He studied how bodies relate to one another, how they interact, and how they affect each other, sometimes pushing towards or apart. He developed wonderful equations that serve to offer some concrete understanding of invisible, yet felt, forces in the physical world.

Here's where you come in.

In order to generate the type of relationship you desire in your life today, it's first essential to diagnose the current status of your relationship, analyze the history of connection dynamics in previous relationships, and set a course toward your ideal relational flow. This process might seem overwhelming if not for a simple theory I use daily with people just like you. It didn't hit me like an apple under a tree but it was essentially the modern equivalent- while sitting before a $5 latte at Starbucks.

The Law of Universal Connection states that no two emotional bodies can remain in a state of disconnection. They will inevitably move toward a state of reparative connection. This is one of those big ideas that rest in basic common sense. We've all been at odds with our partners, family and friends, bosses, etc., and yet even in the worst situations where we feel we will never again speak or care for the other, something starts to change. In certain cases, often as a result of time and space, we just grow less actively angry and resentful, which places us squarely in the realm of repair even though it's unconscious. However, for most cases, we typically gravitate toward repair much faster than we even believe.

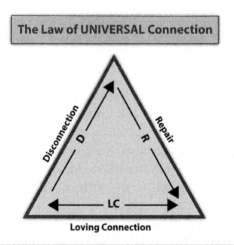

The Law of Universal Connection states that no two emotional bodies can remain in a state of disconnection but will inevitably move toward a state of reparative connection.

Perhaps you can recall being dead center in the midst of a terrible argument with your partner and then giggling out loud at the silliness or absurdity of the moment? Inklings of repair have already begun pulling you back to a state of connection. Most common are those circumstances when a couple really doesn't like one another at the moment, yet there's an energetic pull that subtly leads us back to a state of repair. Perhaps we believe it's just inevitable, or perhaps it is a feeling of helplessness and resignation, yet the reality is that we find ourselves moving back toward a state of connection.

In my experience, all of us are in one of three emotional states at any given point in a relationship. We are either in a state of loving connection, LC, where life is good and we feel like we're loving others and being loved on a regular basis. Or, perhaps, we're in a state of disconnection, D, in which we're in an emotionally distant place where we feel a bit of splintering, cracking, or straining happening due to conflict and discord. And then, there's the state of repair, R, wherein we move toward healing the wound and closing the distance between us. One way or another, we're in a state of Loving Connection, Disconnection, or Repair.

I'm not sure if Sir Isaac Newton believed in unicorns, but I'm almost certain he'd go along with my theory of UniCon. I've found that using the UniCon Ratio is a perfect tool to address all three components of the emotional process in much the same way that Newton used numbers and symbols to quantify the forces of the physical universe.

Remember, much of our feelings about our life, our partners, and the overall state of our relationships can be reduced to a question of perception. How you think and feel makes all the difference in how the general nature of the relationship behaves. The UniCon Ratio is simply a way that we assign percentages to the three sides of the LC-D-R triangle. It's very common for couples to ask me what the "right" or "ideal" split is between Loving Connection, Disconnection, and Repair. I typically respond by pointing out the window and yelling "Look! It's a flying unicorn!" I can offer you my ideal ratio for my own ideal relationship matrix, however it wouldn't be of any service to you in your relationship. This is completely subjective and is largely based upon your childhood examples of relationship, your own personal relationship history, and your vision for your future.

The UniCon Ratio is a ratio to assess and express the movement of connection in your relationship. It's a way to quantify our own insights in our relationships. The first number represents the percentage of time you feel you spend in loving connection with your partner. The second percentage represents the amount of time you spend disagreeing, arguing, or in a general state of disconnection. The third number in the matrix represents the percentage of time you feel you're repairing your relationship and working towards loving connection. The three numbers should total 100% of your time.

% **Loving Connection (LC) – % Disconnection (D) – % Repair (R)**

It's imperative that you not only break down the ratio for your current relationship, but that you also go back in time and analytically rate the average UniCon Ratios for your most important, previous long-term partnerships as well. One of the benefits of this exercise is to give yourself perspective about the nature of your relationship to love and partnership in the past and present and your projection into the future of an ideal ratio.

Also important is the dialogue that ensues once you and your partner have both done this exercise and have prepared your current UniCon Ratio, as well as your ideal ratio. It's fascinating for couples to see how both parties perceive the current state of their relationship, as well as what the fantasies are of the ideal ratio. These perceptions are incredibly useful in terms of creating a deeper understanding for each person and insight into the way they view the nature of the relationship.

For example, a man with a current UniCon Ratio of 15-70-15 has a natural tendency to believe that his relationship is in a constant state of breaking apart and disconnecting. It's not surprising that he has become discouraged and experiences overwhelming feelings of hopelessness due to the belief that he and his partner are always fighting and are always on the rocks. On the other hand, his girlfriend's UniCon Ratio is a 25-10-65. She, understandably, has taken on the role in their partnership of the "fixer." She may feel like someone who constantly initiates communication and healing in the relationship.

Sometimes couples have identical ratios and perceive their relationship to be in the same place. Couples may agree that they're in a good space, that they constantly fight, or that they're always trying to fix things.

An important utilization of the UniCon Ratio is the practice of encouraging partners to experiment with shifting their allocation of energy and focus to create more of what they truly desire. For example, if a woman has a 50% under her Disconnection factor, we discuss what it would take to allocate 10% of that and shift it over to the Repair factor and see what that would be like. A conscious decision to shift the focus of energy over to a different, more enjoyable and functional part of the triangle can translate into a considerable change in the overall loving connection felt between partners.

One of the most important uses of the UniCon Ratio is that it highlights in a tangible way the areas that most require attention and more safety in the relationship. One concrete step in this direction is the creation of Rules of Engagement (RoE). Yes, I know, nobody likes rules. However, these rules work more like agreements and understandings as to how two people intend to act under various circumstances. These rules will help facilitate a sense of security and healthy attachment.

You need rules of engagement when:
- You're not feeling like being close, talking, or interacting.

- You're in the middle of a big argument and it's way past bedtime and one of you wants to go to bed.
- You need to bring up a potentially rough topic with your partner.
- You're feeling disconnected and stuck and want to reconnect but don't know how to do it.
- You want to be intimate but you're feeling uncomfortable initiating after a long dry spell.
- You want to leave a party and you don't want to be rude.
- You want to do virtually anything in the context of your relationship that doesn't come naturally!

Even the best-adjusted, healthiest, most securely attached couples require an understanding as to how things will be conducted in the context of the partnership. Remember, rules of engagement are not expectations — they're working agreements as to how you'll move through the waters of daily life and feel like you still have the security of your partner nearby. It's helpful to use the UniCon Ratio as an assessment tool to identify those areas that need more understanding and focus around engagement than you might've previously anticipated. Once effective RoE are in place, the journey to a higher degree of Loving Connection is far more likely and more easily attainable.

For example, if one person has a significantly large Disconnection factor it's safe to say they're feeling unsafe and frustrated when it comes to reaching for their partner. They may feel like they're mostly there to be supportive and present. What ensues is typically an argument, resentment, anger, and frustration, all of which is usually a cover for the deeper experience of feeling unsafe and detached. It's especially important for this person to communicate with their partner about possible RoE for when these situations arise. Likewise, if a partner has a very low Repair factor in their UniCon Ratio, it's likely they don't consciously allocate a great deal of their energy to healing and reconnecting, which makes the road to Loving Connection all the more challenging! It's crucial to a couple's overall happiness that they sit down and concretely discuss their needs during difficult situations and, most importantly, what they mutually agree to do in future incarnations of that experience.

I encourage couples to take time together following a regular Check-In to discuss your rules of engagement. The discussion begins with an exploration of various "hot spots" in your dynamic together over recent days, weeks, and months. Perhaps you had an argument a few times over the bathroom sink, but it's never really been resolved to the point that it's crystal clear what the protocol is when dealing with the sink. The fights that ensue typically occur as a result of projection and expectation, instead of mutual awareness, which has been translated into a concrete rule of engagement.

Sometimes you might be having what I refer to as a "soft" day where you feel just a little emotional, needy, or insecure. Is it safe to reach for your partner and tell them what you're going through? Why or why not? Has a discussion taken place in which you've made it clear that, while it may be unexplainable or even irrational, you sometimes feel needy and insecure? The process of setting your rules of engagement is a great time to mention that it would mean a lot to you to be able to reach out and feel held emotionally, or even physically, during those soft moments. Another important idea that couples can utilize is the Request for a Reality Check (RRC). By making it part of your agreed upon rules of engagement, you both can simply ask for reassurance with no strings attached or explanations. For example, "I'm feeling low right now and a little anxious about your work thing last night, can I get a reality check, please?" In a partnership where this has been established, the other partner will ideally say: "Baby, I adore you and I am totally here. There's nothing to worry about, but if you need to ask me any questions about last night, I'm open to that."

Another very important Rule of Engagement is the use of Permissions. Unfortunately, it's common for people to take for granted that our partners are always in a position to show up for us simply because they're our partners! Your special person may have had her own long day with ups and downs and may really need a break before showing up for you. Perhaps your special one really wants to watch a TV show. If you start chatting two minutes to start time and become irritated that your partner seems disinterested or keeps checking the clock, it might be a perfect opportunity to insert a permission clause into your RoE. "Is this a good time...?" is a go to phrase in Rules of Engagement and must be relied upon for most conversations that require any length of time or real attention. If you're the sort of partner who walks in from work and starts to dump all the drama from your day out onto the table, you're doing a disservice to both of you as you'll likely not receive the full attention that you deserve and long for and your partner won't receive the respect and appreciation their full attention and support warrants. Attention is not to be taken for granted, but is to be a prime value in relationship. It is, as we discussed earlier, a gift. Presence and full attention is an act of love. Get permission.

One of the most common uses for rules of engagement has to do with disagreements. Even the best of us find ourselves in the Soup. It's fairly unavoidable in human relationships. That said, it isn't necessary for disagreement to derail the process and devolve into utter chaos and serious disconnection. That's where rules of engagement become paramount to the process. Remember, process is a lightning rod that keeps us safe from getting zapped. It's also a safe channel for our interactions even when we're mad, hurt, sad, or feeling the rest of our human emotional palette. Since it's not our problems that get the best of us, but rather our shoddy process, we engage in rules of engagement to make sure we're making decisions based on our higher intention for the relationship, not from the bottom of the soup pot.

Questions to consider while making your Rules of Engagement are:

- What derails us quickly and pushes us out of loving connection?
- What do I need when I'm angry? Hurt? Sad? Afraid? Curious? Lonely? Tired? Hungry?
- What's my responsibility to myself when I experience these emotions?
- What's my partner willing to intend as an agreed upon behavior when I make it clear that I'm feeling a particular emotion or having a particular experience?
- What are the concrete, dependable, and recyclable verbal cues that will trigger the response I need in a particular situation?
- What are our agreements concerning arguing? For example, a time frame or limit to an argument, a request to revisit an argument at an agreed upon further time, a request to enlist the help of a friend or therapist to continue a rough discussion.
- Can I ask for a time out during a bad argument to reestablish that my partner loves me and will not leave, like a Request for Reality Check (RRC)?
- When is it safe to ask for sex? What's our protocol for making intimacy happen? Do we need any rules of engagement for that process?

Renew Your Wows

- The Law of Universal Connection states that no two emotional bodies can remain in a state of disconnection, they will inevitably move toward a state of reparative connection.
- The UniCon Ratio is a ratio to assess and express the movement of connection in your relationship and can help you and your partner identify the different ways you may view your relationship. It can also help you set a shared goal of an ideal UniCon Ratio and, therefore, a mutually satisfying relationship.

- You can use your UniCon Ratio to help you create Rules of Engagement based on each partner's perception of the relationship and unique triggers.
- Rules of Engagement are a useful tool and help keep you grounded in a process paradigm by setting parameters during peaceful times that will help you deal with difficult conversations and situations.

Inspired Actions

1. Figuring the UniCon Ratio. This is a particularly good time to utilize the worksheets found in the Action Guide! As you'll recall, the ratio can be understood as follows:

% Loving Connection (LC) – % Disconnection (D) – % Repair (R)

We're going to figure out three different ratios for the UniCon Ratio. The first ratio will be for your past relationships. The second one will represent your current relationship. Your third ratio will be for your ideal relationship. To begin, identify as many significant long-term relationships that you can reasonably assess retroactively and assign the relationship an average matrix. List each relationship below with the corresponding split. Write down one word or phrase that characterizes the relationship as a whole in the present tense, such as Lovingly Connecting, Disconnecting, Repairing, to the right of the ratio.

An example of an entry might look like this:

Sandra   50-35-15   Connecting but Boring

Bill   15-80-5   Constantly Fighting!

Ok, now your turn! Grab a piece of paper and think about your past relationships. To determine what percentage of your previous relationships that were primarily weighted towards each variable, average each variable. For example, tally up all the Loving Connection percentages, then divide that number by the number of entries. If my 5 Loving Connection percentages were 50%, 30%, 40%, 60%, and 70%, I would add those percentages and get 250. Then, I'll divide 250 by 5 and get the average Loving Connection percentage-

50%. Repeat this for Disconnection and Repair, and write down your average.

Next, assess your current relationship with a UniCon Ratio. How would you qualify the overall experience of your current relationship at this time in one word or phrase?

Now, take a moment and consider the overall experiences from your past relationships, as well as the experience you are having in your current relationship. Consider what has been typical in terms of your UniCon Ratios historically. What's been missing? What have you longed for that you haven't felt satisfied with in the past?

If you had to imagine the ideal relationship scenario, what would it look like? What would it take to get your current relationship to more closely resemble your fantasy? Project an ideal UniCon Ratio into your future and write that down as well.

After you and your partner have completed the previous exercise, take a moment to consider where your current ratio is and where your ideal ratio wants to be. What's one small incremental shift that you can make in order to more closely resemble your ideal relationship dynamic? Try not to adjust anything more than 10% at a time.

Take this opportunity to adjust your current UniCon Ratio and write down your adjusted ratio. Post it somewhere where you can see it daily. For the next week, I encourage you to live from the possibility that this new ratio is completely possible in order to move closer to the relationship you long for.

2. Establish Your Rules of Engagement. Once you've determined the average UniCon Ratio for one another, as well as determined your ideal relationship ratio, i.e. the direction you both wish to move as a team, the next step is devising your RoE. As I mentioned, the need for RoE is not a sign of weakness but rather an indication that the two of you are

realists who desire to live in a state of peace wherein you both get your needs met and feel secure attachment even in rough patches.

Start by discussing what sort of needs arise for you in the course of daily life, as well as in those moments when you find yourself in the Soup. What would help you feel safer, more connected, and hopeful, even when you're feeling challenged?

Next, make a list of intentions, agreements, and/or protocols of behavior during these moments. Identify what the verbal or physical cues are that will trigger the RoE. Make sure both people understand and agree to these RoE and make a copy for both of you to easily reference.

Chapter Eight

Tool 7: Separation of Fact and (Emotional) State

> I can change. I can live out of my imagination instead of my memory.
>
> I can tie myself to my limitless potential instead of my limiting past.
>
> —Stephen Covey

Taking responsibility in a relationship starts with understanding who we are and what we want. It then ultimately follows with agreed upon behavior such as the Rules of Engagement (RoE). This also extends to our past. Many of us hold on to regrets and perceived wrongs done to us in past relationships. But consider this, what if you couldn't blame an ex for a relationship's demise?

Blaming an ex is, at best, a tremendous waste of time and energy and, at worst, a major diversion from doing our own work. Even in situations like infidelity and betrayal, where it's easy to remain angry and continue to feel like a victim, blaming someone is pointless. When we blame someone else, all we're doing is wallowing in how we got hurt and how they did this to us, rather than using it as a learning opportunity. Past relationships teach us that there are no guarantees in relationships. There's likewise no guarantee as to the future of your relationship, whether you're married for decades or newly dating.

Since there are no guarantees, the best approach to the relationship is to give freely as a gift, not as an expectation. Give to the relationship and to your partner because you love them. The moment you start expecting something in return, it's time to stop, utilize awareness, and return to the process. Giving our love as a free gift is part of what makes us happy in relationships. It's not about asking for your partner to meet a particular need. Remember, we don't ask for a need to be satisfied, we express a need. The reality, though, is that if you keep stating your need and your partner is not motivated to meet that need then you either have to fulfill those needs elsewhere or you need to move on.

This is a primary reason people have affairs. Sadly, for the vast majority of people, engaging in an illicit affair isn't an act of getting their needs met, it's an act of anger and aggression. Affairs are typically a distorted approach to meeting a need. Not only do they inevitably lead to the end of the relationship because the partner finds out about it, but the betrayer gets off the hook from actually taking care of their needs in a clean way through the process. They've acted out, leaving betrayal, anger, and animosity in their wake.

You have every right to want to be heard, held, loved or even properly laid. However, acting out isn't the solution. When we're frustrated and worn out from asking for our needs to be met in the same way for months or years, then we're almost surely in denial about what's really going on in our relationship. It's likely a result of a profound lack of felt safety and trust for one or both members of the couple.

This also relates to physical intimacy. Sex is often a symptom, not the core disease in a relationship. In order to feel sexually connected, we need to feel emotionally attached in a safe way. Sex is an outward manifestation of communication, so if our communication isn't going well, chances are our sex life is also suffering. Even in these very difficult moments, it's imperative that we remain clear as to the line between our feelings and what we can establish as facts. The fact may be that your partner has not initiated sex in three weeks but the feeling that they're no longer interested in you is just that, a feeling. It's very important to separate these experiences. Otherwise, you run the risk of projecting your emotional landscape onto your partner and divorcing yourself from the foundation of honest, loving communication that is rooted in personal responsibility.

Our founding father, Mr. Franklin, used his famous treatises for relationships as a way to get his sexual needs met as well as to express his emotional longings. He stipulated in clear terms the conditions under which the sexual exploits would transpire between himself and a lover. He agreed to respond favorably to advances as long as she would do the same. He was also known to write in clauses whereby drinking tea and just hanging out discussing nothing in particular had to be okay. Imagine if you and your partner had a stated agreement that sometimes we "don't have to talk about anything important, including our relationship." This can be your relationship if you're both willing to acknowledge the frustration, resentment, and weariness that has crept into the space between and you both want to do it differently starting *now*, using the process that both Ben Franklin and thousands of couples I've coached have used successfully.

When flowing water meets with obstacles on its path, a blockage in its journey, it pauses. It increases in volume and strength, filling up in front of the obstacle and eventually spilling past it . . .

—I Ching

Imagine trying to back up your iPhone to a stream in the woods that runs into a river and empties out into an ocean. Your brow begins to crease as you dangle your USB cord into the gurgling foam and instead of feeling satisfied and safe that your precious data is secure for another night you notice a welling of condensation on the screen and eventually the device goes gray.

Perhaps this is nothing but a bad dream? In classical dream interpretation, water symbolizes a change of consciousness, literally a *fluid* manifestation of life itself. The idea is that water, like consciousness, flows through our lives and affects us in ways that we sometimes don't comprehend for some time, yet we know there has been a change. Symbolically, we take our phone, filled with ones and zeros, metal and circuitry, and we attempt to identify and relate this machine with safe passage to a flowing manifestation of life itself. This is just a dream, right?

Wrong. We do this every day in our relationships. The attempt to convey information to our partners and have it successfully received, legitimized, and secured is one of our most basic longings as humans. It is also one of the main reasons we tend to complain that we have a problem communicating.

"Facts" and "feelings" are separate entities like brownies and lawnmowers. However, so many couples go off the rails when they conflate the two and speak as if it is *all* one thing.

> *"I feel like you really let me down here. I can't believe you did this to me. What were you thinking? You always do this."*

> *"Yes, I heard you're upset and I'm trying to help you here, but you're shooting down every solution without really considering them, just to spite me. That's what you do. You cry out for help and I can never do anything right for you."*

> *"You always come with me to see my parents and this time you said no, so I assume you're*

*done with my family now? Like, you're too good
for them now, or what?"*

Sound familiar? Disaster! However, it's not a communication problem as much as it is an episode of classic projection rooted in the debacle of facts being merged with feelings. It's extremely likely that one person is discussing their feelings while the other person is discussing facts and vice versa. However, it is also likely that the conscious awareness of separating our needs from expectations is being, on some level, suspended in order to unleash and act out on the fear that we will not be loved. Allow me to explain.

- *The only viable response to an expression of an emotion is an emotionally compatible response.*
- *The only viable response to a discussion of fact is a response that rests in data: ones and zeros.*

Just like a cell phone doesn't speak the same language as a running stream, so it is with emotions and facts. If I'm frustrated about the credit card bill and list expenses hoping to understand what the items represent and you respond by saying I always attack you and that I'm being irrational, our conversation isn't going to end well. If you tell me you feel like you don't really matter to me and my response is to list the number of times in the past week that I've complimented you, our conversation isn't going to end well.

As you can imagine, 1's and 0's (facts) do not safely comingle with hurt and sad (feelings). They're a volatile compound and can blow at any moment. It's incredibly common in partnerships to get messy when it comes to separating facts and feelings. Our feelings can easily drive the bus and when we hand over the keys and take a seat in the back, hoping we get home safe, we're putting the health of our relationship at risk. What's more, this behavior is a prime example of the suspension of personal responsibility when it comes to managing our strong feelings in the face of not getting what we want, when we want it.

If your partner wants to talk about travel plans, it's not likely a great time to talk about your sadness and resentment about not spending enough time together on your last vacation. That's a different, important conversation that will be better served with the RoE. Meeting your partner's invitation to discuss travel plans with the emotional response about unresolved feelings from a previous trip might lead to a foray into the Soup. Instead of hijacking the conversation, use the Process to share your feelings and offer resolution. This could look like: "I'm really excited to plan our trip together, but I feel like I need to process some feelings about the last holiday first or I won't be able to give you my full attention and enthusiasm. Maybe we can table the logistics and schedule some time to talk about my experience from last time first?" Use the seven tools to make yourself and your relationship stronger. That's process played like a baller.

Renew Your Wows

- Understanding who we are and what we want helps us take responsibility for our actions.
- Conversations can turn ugly when one partner is talking about their feelings and the other is talking about facts. Understanding what the conversation is about can help create a more productive dialogue.
- The Rules of Engagement can help provide a backbone for conversations when facts and feelings start to salsa.

Inspired Actions

1. Fact or Feeling? Imagine the person you're in relationship with right now. I want you to take the next 24 hours and breathe into the certainty that this person is God. Maybe you're not big on God, so for you this person might be Michael Jordan, Scarlett Johansen, Warren Buffett, you get the idea. Imagine that your partner is the highest expression of life on the planet. He or she has been sent to you as a messenger of hope, love, and kindness in order to unlock the same within yourself. What do you do with that information? Track the reaction. Do you feel immediately openhearted and excited? Do you feel resistant and skeptical? Angry? Sad? What do you experience and where do you feel it?

Now, consider whether these are facts or feelings. Some of the emotions you might experience when you imagine your partner walking on water can feel profoundly powerful, yet it's likely that you haven't seen this occur in the natural world. Feelings are powerful, they're not facts. On the other hand, it is a fact that your partner makes you coffee every morning and takes the dog out for the early walk because you hate getting up. That's a fact. The feeling of gratitude and appreciation, while it's lovely, is not a fact.

2. Make a Miracles of Daily Life (MDL) list. How open are you to receiving the beauty of your life? Do you anticipate great things when you wake up in the morning or are you waiting for another shoe to drop? What makes you really celebrate? Are the good things coming from inside out or from outside in? Keep this list for one month and then email it or hand it to your partner as a gift of self that you desire to share. It's ok if the list largely reflects the great things your partner is doing for you or highlights the complete absence of

"miracles" you are experiencing as a result of the relationship. Either way, this exercise gives you a chance to track whether you are open to receiving the good things in your life, from where these great things originate, and where they function in the relationship. More than anything, the list is a conversation starter with your partner and can lead to an opening of personal sharing for you both.

Chapter Nine

I Follow the Process and I'm Still Not Happy

I have heard what the talkers were
talking, the talk of the beginning and the end,

But I do not talk of the beginning or the end.

There was never any more inception than there is now,

Nor any more youth or age than there is now,

And will never be any more
perfection than there is now,

Nor any more heaven or hell than there is now.

Urge and urge and urge,

Always the procreant urge of the world.
— Walt Whitman, Song of Myself

During World War 2, it became popular to describe planes on bombing runs that barely made it back to base intact as limping home on one wing and a prayer. So many couples seem to feel this way, as if they barely know how the relationship made it another day, week, or even a year. What a way to live! Yet, we seem to easily distract ourselves with our partner's behaviors and shortcomings often becoming oblivious to our own ups and downs. Relationships are chartered by two co-pilots, each of which is responsible for their own self-analysis, introspection, and personal development. Imagine one pilot who constantly takes continuing education classes, seeks ongoing training and review, because they want to be the best pilot they can be. What if the co-pilot has a tendency to flick on the cruise control and play Words With Friends?

Consider this: This isn't a relationship problem, it's a personal preference. Forget why your partner is who they are and forget trying to get them to change. Focus on you. Why do you get upset and critical? Why do you historically choose co-pilots who have little interest in doing continuing education and pursuing ongoing training? What will it take to be joyful and will it be helped or hindered on this current flight with this person sharing the cockpit?

Finding the right person is a "to do" item on everyone's list, but it's a myth. I don't believe we simply find the right person. It's more about whether we're open to relationship or not.

Sometimes drawing someone into our lives can be as easy as shifting some aspect of the way we are living. Before I met my wife I learned I had to make space for another person in my house. I was living alone in a three-bedroom apartment and there was just no space for anybody else. I had art everywhere, my closets were full, and there was only one night table. After hearing Katherine Woodward Thomas speak at a local event about "Calling in the One," I went home and took down anything that reminded me of ex-girlfriends, even the ones I still liked. I spent hours assembling the requisite Ikea night table for my unknown, future special lady. I made space in my closets. Not more than a week later, I met my wife. It was amazing.

Instead of asking what kind of partner you need, try asking what kind of partner you want to be and create that energetic shift. Oprah made popular the idea of writing out a list of all the qualities and attributes you feel your partner needs to have and putting that up on a vision board - everything from hair color to matching socks. However, I encourage people to take all of that energy and put it back into themselves by asking: "What kind of qualities do I want to exude?" If you're putting a certain energy out, this is essentially what you will draw back. But if you're pointing to a description of what another person has to offer, what are you really suggesting? You're not offering anything, you're just saying, "This is what I require." If I'm your partner, I want someone who's going to meet me in the middle; I don't want somebody who's going to want more than I have to offer.

When I see somebody who keeps going to dating events trying to find the "right" person, I find it's usually because they have more work to do in themselves, rather than their inability to find the right person.

If this is happening to you, it's time to ask:

Where am I blocked? Where is my work?

What are my limitations and what am I doing about them?

While I believe people can change to meet someone's needs, it has to start with strong desire from within. The great theologian, Paul Tillich, claimed that *boredom is rage spread thin*. Basically, we tend to numb out and claim to be bored when we're actually feeling quite a lot underneath and feel overwhelmed when we consider what it'll take to actually change things. Sometimes we feel exhausted, as if we just don't have the energy to care what happens in the relationship. Consider how much energy it takes to keep anger safely tucked inside, quiet and controlled? It's exhausting. Actually expressing the anger and resentment we feel in a relationship typically comes early on. It might be when you've gotten quiet, disconnected, and "tired" that the actual truth of the situation has come to a head.

For example, recall the case of the woman who kept saying to her husband, "Why can't you meet my needs? Why can't you just give me what I want?" – to which her husband would reply, "I don't know what the hell you are talking about." What if he'd said, "Sweetie, I'll do whatever it takes to give you whatever you want. Just have patience with me. I'm working on it." Hearing this, most of us would stick around because we feel like our partner wants to meet our needs, wants to understand us, and wants to love us the way we want to be loved.

Similarly, if someone states that they're not able to meet your needs or that you're asking for too much, it's time to consider whether or not that's the picture that you want. Most of us would rather be with someone who is striving to meet our needs, not telling us they're unwilling or unable to meet them. If you've searched within yourself and found that what you're asking for is reasonable and you're receiving a response like this from your partner, it may be a warning sign that this relationship is not working for you.

Rather than trying to squeeze a triangle into a square, it's much easier to be with someone where you'll feel nurtured, loved, and adored, than with someone that *might* get there one day. Living in the future, always hoping someone will change or live up to their potential, can be a long road to bitterness and resentment and probably speaks more to your sense of "deservability." I always recommend making that exploration before you're in that situation.

Interestingly, the greatest illusion I see about a "right" partner exists primarily in people who claim to have never found their partner or only found disappointment in relationships by middle age. For example, I have known so many women in their 30s, 40s, and 50s, who are frustrated and angry that life has not *given them* the right partner.

It's not about waiting for the right partner to come or molding someone into the person you want. Mold yourself.

Act in the way you want a partner to act towards you, and you'll probably have a much easier time in finding the right person. Become the picture and be the right partner.

Letting Go of the Picture

> **Let the waters settle.**
> **You will see stars and moon mirrored in your Being.**
>
> —Rumi

In being the right partner, some of the most fruitful questions to explore are:
- What am I bringing, what am I creating?
- What space am I meeting the other in?
- Am I encountering this person as an extension of myself?
- Am I meeting in a space that we share?
- What do I expect to gain from this as opposed to being open to whatever happens?
- Am I enjoying this moment knowing that I have no control over it?
- Am I trying to elicit a response from you and that's why I'm choosing the words that I'm choosing?

It's a fairly simple and straightforward concept. We know in our minds when we're judging or viewing someone else based on what we expect versus who they are. What can be challenging, though, is letting go of that picture of what someone *should* be. In a relationship, holding onto these distorted pictures leads to disappointment, hurt, and resentment.

For many people it's a hard process to get to the space of letting go of the picture. Part of the problem we have is that our culture, media, films, and books condone it. The other day I was reading a string of comments on Facebook about *50 Shades of Grey*. There were a number of women saying,

"Who's your Christian Grey?" They'd then enumerate celebrities and post their pictures. They've created, quite publicly, a picture of expectations for their future partners. To be clear, I'm not picking on women here. Men do the same thing.

That's not process, that's either/or. It's transaction. And unfortunately, it's quite common. There's definitely a relationship between that kind of thinking and what shows up in our relationship when we project that into the relationship. This can be hurtful to our partners and our relationship.

And I don't think it's getting any better given the times we live in. With the advent of the Internet, it's very common for people to form and develop online relationships with people they have never met. We can create incredibly deep attachments to people based on responses to e-mails and texts that we receive, that aren't based on daily life together or interactions in real time. Often the intensity we feel for those whom we've never had the pleasure of sharing a meal with in real life is a complete projection onto that person. It's more about who we want them to be than who they are.

Being able to see this is easier once you have clarity around, or awareness of, your own projection. If I have feelings for somebody and am willing to quit my job and move across the country to be with them, without ever having met them in person, what is that really saying? What does it say about me and what I've created?

Letting go of the picture is liberating. It's freeing to accept that although we have pictures in our mind of what we want, being present for whomever and wherever somebody is, is our true goal.

On Marriage

It's important to briefly address the institution of marriage, as many of you will be reading this from your marital bed, your marital car, or your maritally shared iPad.

Often we complain that the person we're married to isn't the same person we married. But why would you want to be with the same person that you married 10 years ago? You aren't the same person you were 10 years ago. Part of the beauty of a relationship is growing, changing, and learning, and having yourself reflected through your partner's eyes. This is one of the greatest gifts.

That being said, if you choose a partner with so many unfinished parts, a partner who requires more handholding than you have the space to hold or accept, it might be painful, but the best move for both of you may be to consider a break.

But what if you're already married? Let's face it, it takes an incredible amount of courage and real commitment to heal the hurt places sometimes, but we owe it to ourselves to do it. If your partner constantly reflects back to you that you're just too broken for them, it's going to be frustrating and depressing and you probably won't get your needs met. It's better to let them know now than to continue fantasizing about what you hope for in the future. After all, if they can't meet your basic needs today, better communication probably isn't the issue. It might simply be that we aren't well matched right now. Sometimes part of learning is knowing when to move on.

Many therapists go down the road of trying to take the relationship in front of them, and do whatever they can to keep people together. This has never been my strategy. My approach is to raise awareness, clarity, and communication for couples so they can make a meaningful decision for themselves as to whether the relationship still serves them. Even in cases of marriage.

What, then, is success?

> *In a successful relationship, you have learned*
> *how to express your needs and desire to meet*
> *your partners' needs freely without expectation,*
> *until it becomes a seamless expression of love,*
> *respect and appreciation. Success is existing*
> *together in a paradigm that supports healthy*

attachment and safe connection all in
the present moment.

If a relationship truly grows as an extension of each other and supports each other's growth, then in my book, do it as long as you can. Relationships of this caliber are sadly rare. Staying together for 50 years just because you can isn't really much of an accomplishment. Staying together because it brings you immense joy and satisfaction; because you deeply desire the connection, is.

In order for marriage to be relevant as an institution in the 21st century, it must be revolutionary. It's only as spiritual and meaningful as the partners who comprise the coupleship. Marriage is not a magic cloak that disguises the status quo and miraculously transforms two people who're not willing to work and aren't at their core loving and kind with one another.

Revolution is the only solution to resurrect the saliency of marriage. Revolt against stale understandings of love and a tolerance for laziness and a lack of responsibility. Stop hiding behind your marriage licenses and push yourselves to thrive. Risk loving from a place of not knowing it all.

If It Ends

The real epidemic in our country isn't just heart disease or diabetes; it's loneliness and depression and isolation.

— Dean Ornish

When clients are going through a rough period in their relationship, one of the first things I encourage is to truly feel the pain, anger, hopelessness, frustration, sadness, and whatever other emotions might be present. This isn't always easy as it can be quite a challenge to allow ourselves to sit in a state of discomfort. Yet, in my experience, avoiding the feelings typically leads to an encore performance down the road. If I won't feel it now, I'll likely have the opportunity to feel it again later. In this situation, it's essential to ask ourselves what we're truly feeling and what opportunities for growth those emotions may present to us. We can use the process to learn more about our selves, our needs, and how we can respond in this situation.

Still, we must return always to our key question, "Who do I want to be?" Do I want to be the person who feels a loss of love or connection, clouds up, and rains all over my partner making them bad and wrong? Or, do I want to evolve into the sort of person who takes a deep breath and assesses what's truly in my best interest. Do we remove all of our money out of the 401K every time the stock market drops out? Well, some of us do. Yet, the conventional wisdom would be to look at the bigger picture. Why am I in the market to begin with? Long-term gains outweigh the short-term losses. Same thing goes in our intimate partnerships. If we were to pack our bags each time the going gets rough, then what's our long-term game? If many of us want the sense of security in truly having a mate who knows us, stands with us in good times and bad, and wipes our ass when we're no longer able to make sense of toilet paper rolls then the long-term game is the only game to be played here.

We've evolved from beings of war to beings of peace. Likewise, our relationships must evolve from a physical dynamic of fight or flight to an art form of conscious awareness to our inherent biology, our innate tendency to attack or run, and craft a more effective, more loving approach to coping with our fear. Relationship as art is about playing the long game. It's about mastering the art of your life without fighting because you don't have what you want or running away to find it somewhere else. Unless, of course, this time your biology got it right. In this case, Fight or Flight is on.

Because marriage is a "pretend" vessel, it can end – even though many people believe that if we get married, we have some kind of failsafe that our relationship can't, or won't, end.

Marriage is an attempt to concretize that which can't be solidified. There may come a beautiful, but painful, moment when you realize that you're with a partner that doesn't meet your needs.

There's an awareness that's very sobering, sometimes sad, sometimes freeing, that it's not about my partner being a bad person, it's just about my partner being themselves in a way that doesn't serve me. Whether your partner can't or won't meet your needs or whether we no longer care about meeting our partner's needs, coming to awareness about the true state of the relationship is a gift that will allow you and your partner to move on in a safer, healthier way.

Remember, you don't need your partner in order to feel good about yourself. When you think back to the "good times" and how great it was to feel alive, I want to make it completely clear that you felt alive not because your partner made you feel that way but because you felt so comfortable and safe to be yourself that you were willing to access your own bliss and truth.

As the great Eve Eschner Hogan comments in her book *The Eros Equation*, "recognizing that it wasn't the other person who caused your feelings of love — but rather that you merely accessed your own source of love — can help you recognize that the love didn't go away when that person left or disappointed you. You just closed the door again. The other person never held the key in the first place; he or she just activated your choice to love."

It's only when you're willing to stop projecting the mountain of "greatness" onto your partner that you can truly appreciate the gifts they offered without seeing them as necessities required to be who you really are. They are invitations to rise to the surface of your pond of brilliance but they do not make your pond brilliant. You will survive and even more now that you have a recent memory and emotional frequency of how it felt to be in that magical place of love and you will be very tuned in when you experience once again those same feelings welling up inside of you.

Renew Your Wows

- Instead of focusing on some ideal type of partner, consider what kind of partner you want to be and move toward that being.
- Let go of that picture of the perfect someone. There is no "right" person.
- A successful relationship is one in which you can express your needs and give freely without expectation, until it no longer serves both of you – if and when it no longer serves you.
- If your relationship no longer serves your needs or the needs of your partner, utilizing the process can help you come to an amicable end and be grateful for the time you had together.

Inspired Actions

1. Track your dreams. In ancient Greece, dream incubation rites were commonly used as a way to understand what was making us sick or sad, stuck or blind, when it came to our lives. The god Asklepios, who would go on to symbolize our modern medical field with his staff and serpents, would come to people in their sleep and tell them what to do in order to heal. The roads to and from the temples were piled with crutches and slings, left by folks who successfully received their prescriptions in their sleep.

Our dreams aren't often prescriptive, but at the very least they are reflective. Keep a dream journal and notice what's going on when you drift off into the realm of your unconscious. The dreams we dream can be understood as our unconscious self attempting to communicate with our conscious self. Consider what the prevailing feelings in your dream are. Is your partner present? How about your parents? Are there recurring themes? Do you wake up anxious, sad, angry, or distant from your partner?

2. Is it time to seek counseling? Start with a session or two for yourself. From there you can get a sense from the therapist whether individual work or couples work is better for your situation. Remember, it's important to be open to the possibility that you might need to hit the abort button on your relationship, but it's also vital to your future peace and calm to know that you did everything in your power to heal the wounds and learn better processes before you terminate the coupleship.

3. Make a list of everything you can do to be loving and kind to your partner and a list of everything you can think of to be loving and kind to yourself. Weigh both of these lists and

determine whether they are contraindicated or if they can co-exist in a way that feels comfortable for you.

Conclusion

Check-In Now or Check Out Later

> The very least you can do in your life is to figure
> out what you hope for. And the most you can do is live
> inside that hope. Not admire it from a distance but
> live right in it, under its roof.
>
> — Barbara Kingsolver

Taking control of your relationship today is about reclaiming your relationship with yourself. Simply hoping that things will work themselves out because there's so much love between you and your partner distracts you from one of the great truths of life. Coupling is about two individuals and the degree to which they know themselves and are willing to share themselves with their partner in the context of a healthy, safe attachment. The work of relationship is the work of two people doing their own inner journey so they can show up for the shared, outer journey.

There's no question that renewing your wows in your current relationship or any other requires constant attention. Of course, there are days when you just don't feel like it. Perhaps you haven't quite let go of something they said or did the day or week before, or perhaps you had a bad dream the night before where you watched your partner have sex with other people. If you're like most people, this will no doubt cause a change in flow when you wake up the next morning, causing a feeling of disconnect. This is perfectly normal and understandable. Even so, it's a choice as to how you will play this out throughout the day.

One of the greatest pieces of the puzzle we've uncovered in this book is the power of mindset and intention when it comes to healthy relationships. There are moments when you simply have to overcompensate for a drop in cabin pressure, so to speak, by breaking out the champagne and holding an impromptu celebration. When you feel disconnected for no apparent reason, have a party and dance your partner around the room. This is no different than performing a random act of kindness for a perfect stranger other than the fact that you *adore* the person you're celebrating with. An unconditional act of kindness, appreciation, or celebration – especially when you feel out of flow – makes the statement to yourself that, "This is what I want, what I choose for my life, and I'm willing to make this investment to ensure that it's incredible and meaningful."

If you're looking for a sign that this person before you is the right partner for you, then you've most likely lost your center. To return to a state of alignment, peace, and joy, focus on going deeper within. No partner is ever going to be right unless you feel right in your own being.

By this point, you should have a pretty good answer to my original question, "Who are you and what do you want?" It doesn't need to be your final answer, it just needs to be a working answer – something you can run the program with and see how it feels.

As you gain a deeper understanding of yourself, you'll find that showing up in your relationship feels different. If the result of knowing yourself and seeing the dance of your own reactions and your unique part of the negative cycle makes you feel more distant from your partner, then it might be time to check in, connect, and go even deeper. Taking the risk of vulnerability by sharing the awareness that you're feeling guarded, sad, or resentful is part of the best you can offer in any relationship. When it comes to renewal, you must first be conscious about what you are renewing, as well as where you want to go once you've exfoliated what no longer serves you from the past.

When you look across at your partner, do you see someone that lives inside your dream? Perhaps today it's a faint glimpse of what you will eventually create in the space between one another. Yet, what a tremendous gift it is to know that you now have a process that'll serve you each step of the way, regardless of whatever bumps in the road you may encounter. One of the greatest gifts you give yourself and your partner is the beauty of showing up in all of your glory, strengths, and vulnerabilities. Remember, if you find yourself in the Soup, it takes two people to get out of it. However, all it takes is one of you to take lead on the journey back. If you want to reconnect and reclaim a safe alliance then make it safer. Take steps to make it a smooth path back to the space between the two of you.

If you're feeling frustrated and resentful that it's taking so darn long for your partner to return to you then it's most likely also true that your partner is questioning your vulnerability and safety. On the other hand, if brushing off some layers has revealed a more confident and loving you, it's likely that you've already begun to perceive your partner in a more positive, hopeful way. In order to renew your wows, it's imperative that you renew your faith in yourself and your ability to exist in a healthy, loving partnership. When you know yourself, you have a better sense about what you want and how you want to go about getting it.

How do you know if the relationship is really not working? Well, it doesn't feel good for one thing. That's the obvious clue, yet it may not feel so obvious once you accept that we oftentimes push our partners away because of how they challenge our deep retooling and growth. Still, if you ask yourself what your top three non-negotiables are and they are being met less than 50% each, you may be in a relationship that will never meet your needs in the way you desire. Non-negotiables are meant to be met, not compromised. If you're compromising on what you feel you must have in your life, no matter whom you're with, in order to feel complete and aligned, then there is a strong chance that you will move through your days angry and uncomfortable that you are somehow selling yourself short. You might come to feel that you're *submerging* your true nature rather than *emerging* as the radiant being you know yourself to be. This can't stand.

If you truly feel like you're submerging yourself and preventing real personal growth, there has never been a better time to use the process illustrated in this book, even if it's for a conscious, loving break-up. Needs instead of expectations, responses instead of reactions, and noticing your partner as a unique other are all signs of respect that offer some dignity to the end of a once special relationship. If you're unable to renew your wows, then at least take some classy bows. Spend some real time reminiscing together about the good days and the great memories. Offer your words of appreciation and make them heartfelt. You don't need to end a relationship with anger, blame, and big fits of drama in order to feel like it's done. Once you both know it's ending, make it a commitment to end it well. The manner in which we end a relationship has a significant bearing on how the next relationship begins.

The concepts and tools in this book are here for you as a way to establish a healthy process together, one that supports a positive sense of attachment, built on emotional safety, and funneled through a tried and true, agreed upon system of rules of engagement. Your process is your lifeline. Treat it with respect and gratitude so that when things hit the fan, there's no question as to "what happens when" in order to get out of the Soup in a timely, less painful fashion. When you know there's emotional distance between the two of you, state it out loud, not as a complaint, but as an invitation.

Use the exercises in this book to reclaim your safe attachment when it feels like the soup is on the stove. Get permission from your partner, make an appointment, and initiate a check-in as soon s possible. Start with the beautiful appreciations you feel, especially when you have to push yourself through the resistance and fear. Be honest and vulnerable when you offer your need to feel connected and safe. Give the gift of doing more of the heavy lifting when it comes to finding the sweet spot again between I and Thou. You'll renew your wows when you renew your conscious awareness that you're simply in a temporary state of distance. The contrast of knowing what you want and seeing where you are at this moment will give you the roadmap. The tools in this book will give you the process required.

Enlightenment in the context of relationship is all about the state of peace and acceptance we experience while we're in the Soup with our friend, lover, or even a family member. It's easy to feel enlightened when we're shrouded in the light of loving kindness and reciprocated connection. Far more challenging it is, says Yoda, to bring the light into the darkness without expectation that night will instantly turn to day.

One of our main tasks when we feel stuck is to remember that we're only in a temporary state of agitation and disconnect, but that, as in all things, the cycle of life and death is a constant loop. This too shall pass and we will once again feel excited and alive to the point where we notice our own growth, as well as the growth of our partner, in a new paradigm of mutual respect and appreciation.

It's who we are as humans to want to love and be loved. It's also quite common to act in ways that make this offering and acquisition dance quite an enigma for many of us. It doesn't need to be as daunting as we tell ourselves if we adhere to the cornerstone of a healthy process. Remember, you're both truly trying to connect and feel safe.

My challenge to you today is to start practicing the ideas and tools described in this book without waiting for your partner to do so. You must first fully understand and make a deep connection with who *you* are and how you truly want to walk in the world separate from any expectation or demand that your partner, or anyone else, will change. The gift you give your relationship is to celebrate your relationship to your Self first and then allow that conscious, aligned being to reach out and offer itself to another aligned being in a perfect I-Thou moment.

It's my deepest desire that the words on these pages be used to reclaim your birthright of healthy, safe attachment in your relationships. You don't have to suffer, but you do need to take responsibility for who you are, what you want, and how you'll get there.

Praise for the Process

Each building block created a higher sense of partnership, an "I-Thou" dynamic, rather than "me vs. you" where either side dictates expectations of the other without considering the couple. The absence of expectations, coupled with the expression of needs, as facilitated by "check ins," was difficult at first, but ultimately, helped us to understand each other and work towards helping each other, rather than disappointing each other.

Jeffrey's been a marriage saver. His easy demeanor and honest approach has led us to a better place and a better understanding of ourselves and ourselves as a couple. A few simple tweaks and we were back on track and growing together, rather than apart.

—Sue Ann

You saved my marriage with the guidance and techniques you provided. I am simply amazed at how much better we are at communication and conflict resolution. Although we've had to work through some very painful moments, we have always found our way through using the methods that you taught us. We continue to do our Check-In every weekend and it has become a loving ritual that we both look forward to.

We talk to each other now much like we did when we first met. We have become the loving and tender partners we always dreamed of. These are such simple words to say, but the daily effort to achieve them is ongoing, yet welcome. The work that we have done has impacted all parts of our life- other relationships, and even work, seem to go so much more smoothly. I can't thank you enough for your help. My life has never been better.

—Evvie

We quickly realized after only a couple of sessions with you that we needed to do some strong soul searching and self-evaluation before we could even consider starting a family, let alone repair our marriage. We benefited most by your ability to get us to open up and be honest with each other. Your ability to get me to talk about thoughts and feelings, most of them for the first time, helped me open up and exponentially expanded our connection to each other.

—Tom

You made it clear from the beginning that there was no guarantee of a repaired marriage. Setting that expectation aside really helped us form a base to look at ourselves as individuals first, before looking at ourselves as part of a couple. The Check-In is a useful tool that forced me to initiate situations I was not normally comfortable with. It created an intimate time for us to disconnect from the crazy realities of the day and focus on each other. Honestly, at times, we didn't have to run through the three steps of the Check-In to get the benefit of it. We often used the time to say nice and endearing thoughts to each other.

—Colleen

We were challenged throughout our pregnancy process. I feel strongly that the time we spent in counseling really helped us with our reaction and responses. Getting pregnant was not an easy task for us and being there for each other was a must. Understanding each other's emotions and responding to them in a positive and supportive manner helped the process become a connection, rather than another challenge.

We'll be put to the test again going forward while raising our bundle of joy, but we're armed with love and the tools we've learned, and now look forward to changes and challenges. We know we can work through them and come out stronger as a couple and individuals.

—Steven

Jeffrey was a truly compassionate guide for my wife and me. He listened carefully and challenged us to reconsider assumptions we'd made about each other that we weren't even fully aware of. He provided concrete strategies for improving communication and an ongoing plan to continue our work after our sessions ended. In particular, he helped us change the way we talk to each other. We're now more comfortable, direct, and loving when we discuss difficult issues, because we've replaced old habits of confrontation with a real feeling of partnership.

— Brian

Jeffrey and his process took us from the verge of divorce and brought us back to a loving place. Like so many couples, we couldn't communicate or share ourselves and our feelings on a personal level. He helped us strip away most of our triggers, and revealed a process of identifying reactions vs. responses that's led us to better communication. When you slow down and respond to your partner, it becomes much easier for them to realize that you're listening and care about what his needs are. It also stops the Ping-Pong arguing, where you both volley points back and forth and cast blame, rather than working through a problem to its mutually beneficial solution.

— Eileen

We've learned to recognize each other's innate expressions of love now that we have distinguished what they are. The thing that has lasted the longest is the conversation we had where we talked about how each of us experiences feeling loved. I am not a particularly emotional gal and show my love by taking care of my partner and our lives together. However, he prefers to experience love via emotion, and doesn't see my gestures and the effort I put into our lives together as me expressing my love for him. Now, we each make an effort to express love in the way the other person likes to be loved. I make an effort to make emotional statements of love and he makes an effort to take care of me.

— Heleen

References

Ardagh, Arjuna. *Better Than Sex: The Ecstatic Art of Awakening Coaching.* Awakening Coaching, LLC. 2013.

Bowlby, John. *The Making and Breaking of Affectional Bonds.* Routledge, 1979.

Brach, Tara Ph.D. *Radical Acceptance: Embracing Your Life With the Heart of a Buddha.* Bantam. 2004.

Buber, Martin. *Between Man and Man (Routledge Classics).* Routledge. 2002.

Buber, Martin. *I and Thou.* (Walter Kaufman, *trans.*) Touchstone. 1971.

Deida, David. *The Way of the Superior Man: A Spiritual Guide to Mastering the Challenges of Women, Work, and Sexual Desire.* Sounds True. 2004.

Ecenbarger, William. Benjamin Franklin: Ben Franklin's Dangerous Liaisons. *The Chicago Tribune,* 1990.

Franklin, Benjamin. *The Autobiography of Benjamin Franklin (Dover Thrift Editions).* Dover Publications. 1996.

Gottman, John. *Seven Principles for Making Marriage Work.* Crown. 1999.

Hanh, Thich Nhat. *Reconciliation: Healing the Inner Child.* Parallax Press. 2010.

Hendrix, Harville Ph.D. *Getting The Love You Want: A guide for couples.* Holt. 1988.

Hogan, Eve Eschner. *Intellectual Foreplay: Questions for Lovers and Lovers to Be.* Hunter House. 2000.

Hogan, Eve Eschner. *The Eros Equation: A "Soul-ution" for Relationships*. Hunter House. 2014.

Jetha, Cacilda and Ryan, Christopher. *Sex At Dawn: How We Mate, Why We Stray, and What It Means for Modern Relationships*. Harper. 2012.

Johnson, Susan M. *Hold Me Tight: Seven conversations for a lifetime of love*. Little, Brown. 2008.

Johnson, Susan M. *The Practices of Emotionally Focused Couple Therapy: Creating connection*. Brunner/ Routledge, 2004.

Jung, Carl Gustav. *The Collected Works of C.G. Jung, Vol. 9, Part 1: The Archetypes and the Collective Unconscious* (Bollingen Series, No. 20). Princeton University Press. 1969.

Jung, Carl Gustav. *The Symbollic Life: Miscellaneous Writings (The Collected Works of C.G. Jung, Vol. 18)*. Princeton University Press. 1977.

Jung, Carl Gustav. *The Undiscovered Self (Jung Extracts, Book 20)*. Princeton University Press. 1990.

Jung, Carl Gustav. *The Undiscovered Self, reprint, reissue*. Signet. 2006.

Ladinsky, Daniel, (trans). *The Gift: Poems by Hazif, The Great Sufi Master*. Penguin. 1999.

Real, Terrence. *The New Rules of Marriage: What You Need to Know to Make Love Work*. Ballantine. 2008.

Schnarch, Dr. David. *Intimacy & Desire: Awaken The Passion In Your Relationship*. Beaufort. 2009.

Schnarch, David. *Passionate Marriage: Love, Sex, and Intimacy in Emotionally Committed Relationships*. W.W. Norton & Company. 1997.

Thomas, Katherine Woodward. *Calling in "The One": 7 Weeks to Attract the Love of Your Life*. Harmony. 2004.

Tipping, Colin. *Radical Forgiveness: A Revolutionary Five-Stage Process to Heal Relationships, Let Go of Anger & Blame, Find Peace in Any Situation*. Sounds True, Inc. 2009.

Watts, Alan. *This Is It: And Other Essays on Zen and Spiritual Experience.* Random House. 1958.

Welwood, John. *Perfect Love, Imperfect Relationships: Healing the Wound of the Heart.* Trumpeter. 2006.

Williamson, Marianne. *A Return to Love: Reflections on the Principles of A Course in Miracles.* Harper Collins. 1996.

Appendix

Please download your complimentary companion workbook using the following link:

Renew Your Wows Action Guide:
A Workbook of Relatable Proportions

http://www.jeffreysumber.com/ryw-action-guide

Acknowledgements

> I don't believe people are looking for the meaning of life as much as they are looking for the experience of being alive.
> —Joseph Campbell

I feel so blessed to have the experiences of my life, past, present, and future. What a ride it has been.

Thanks Mom and Dad for being amazing teachers regarding relationships. You have offered different models for partnership throughout my life and provided a wonderful assortment of templates from which to choose. Sitting together with my dad editing this book brought me back to editing high school English papers. I'm so blessed and grateful to have had so many such moments with you, Dad. You're so sharp, yet kind and soft! Mom, you taught me so many times to do my best and trust that it'll work out. "What's the worst that can happen…" became a rallying cry that helped accomplish this book. Thank you for your tenacity and your generosity, always.

Daniel and Jonathan, thank you for being great brothers. Your friendship has made the difficulties of life smoother with your ability to always make me laugh and appreciate the common bond we share. You sweeten the best moments with kindness and sincerity like no others.

I am grateful to my friends and family for their constant support and belief in who I am. I thank all of the clients, students, and couples throughout the years that have elected to work together in the unfolding process and have shared their insights and struggles in the name of life and love so that we might all thrive in our relationships. Your hard work is a huge part of this book and I'm indebted to all of you for sharing your vulnerability and living in the Process.

I am overwhelmed with gratitude for my wife, Kari, for her endless gift of acceptance, her decision to allow a co-pilot in her cockpit, and her faithful reminder to simply "be nice." There is a strong case to be made for including her as a co-author as I never would have had the opportunity to fine tune my process without her beautiful presence in my life, challenging me to step out of the Soup and into the kitchen. Thank-you, Noodle, for your incredible patience, overwhelming good nature, and your sweet laugh.

Gratitude goes to great coaches, Eve Hogan, Barb Heenan, and Scott Armstrong. Special thanks to my writing team: Mathes Sclafani, Kim Burger, and Tania Brown. Thank-you to Mrs. DelCampo for being the best 10th grade English writing teacher a guy could have. Thanks to Jamie for saving the day by getting me covered and to Danielle Camorlinga for the matches idea.

Kudos to those who stepped out of the bubble to endorse and support this book beyond the traditional path.

Gratitude to Jerry Jud, Lawrence Stibbards, Joy Davey, Jerome Bernstein, Steve Martz, Naomi Hannah, Dr. Sue Johnson, Katherine Ninos, Arnold Mindell, Harville Hendrix, Shalom Mountain, IPEC, Eve Hogan, John Duffy, Benu, Annette Tacconelli, Jana, Cira, Birch, Pamela, Vered, Trixie, Andy, Bruce, Clementine, Janna, Maxim, Binah, Chaco, Tashi, Shelby, Nirbo, Michelle, The Nameless One, Joy, Troy, Anna, Andrea, Howard, Barb and Haydn, Hermit, Karen, Eli, Sharon, Roy, Alexa, Mary Catherine, Maria, Kimmie, Mary, Yesi, Zwartburger, Katy and Jay, Nancy, Natalie, Roseann,

Liz, Lisa, Steve, Susan, Peggy, Tom, Roberto, Julie, Rome, Molly, Claudia, Cara and Lisa, Trixie, and Kimmie Kim.

Thank-you to the lame therapists as well, for teaching me what does not work for folks on the couch and what not to do from the armchair.

About the Author

Jeffrey Sumber is a highly sought-after psychotherapist, life coach, and relationship consultant in practice for almost twenty years. He has worked passionately to help couples that are struggling to see themselves in a new light and adopt unique approaches to communication. Jeffrey's proven approach to relationships has provided the powerful intervention, direction, and support needed to help thousands of couples "renew their wows."

After receiving degrees from Colgate and Harvard, he traveled the world studying with master teachers, psychoanalysts, shamans, entrepreneurs, and relationship experts. Mentored by relationship greats such as Harville Hendrix, Jerry Jud, Arnold Mindell, Lawrence Stibbards, Wayne Dyer, Dr. Sue Johnson, and Eve Hogan, Jeffrey formulated his own process- a synthesis between classical transpersonal psychology and contemporary approaches to relationships, such as Imago and Emotionally Focused Therapy (EFT).

Mr. Sumber is a highly recognized professional when it comes to love, relationship and social psychology. He speaks frequently on the topic of conscious coupling in the media, has made appearances on TLC's Four Weddings reality show, and on Huffington Post Live. His website **www.JeffreySumber.com** and newsletters are a constant source of information and inspiration for couples everywhere and his interviews on top psychology, news, and social websites continue to keep his expertise a high-value target for those who want to make living mindfully and happily a matter of daily practice. He's a regular blogger and communicates with the public daily through Facebook and Twitter.

Jeffrey is practical, solution-focused, irreverent, yet professional, and is always interested in the overall healing and healthy process of the people with whom he interacts. He currently lives in Chicago, Illinois with his beloved wife, Kari, with whom he constantly strives to be the best partner imaginable.

Known internationally for his unique writing, workshops, and coaching on relationships, personal growth, and intimacy, Jeffrey Sumber makes the often confusing and maddening corridors of interpersonal dynamics clear and concrete. His development of The Process as a lightning rod for couples allows you a sense of safety (even when you are in the "Soup") without diminishing your unique circumstances.

In order to work directly with Jeffrey Sumber, please contact him at his website, **www.JeffreySumber.com** in order to schedule private counseling, coaching or consultation appointments.

DISCARD

CPSIA information can be obtained at www.ICGtesting.com
Printed in the USA
LVOW04s0556290815

452025LV00019B/1140/P

9 780996 311106